A Woman's
Amazing
Grays

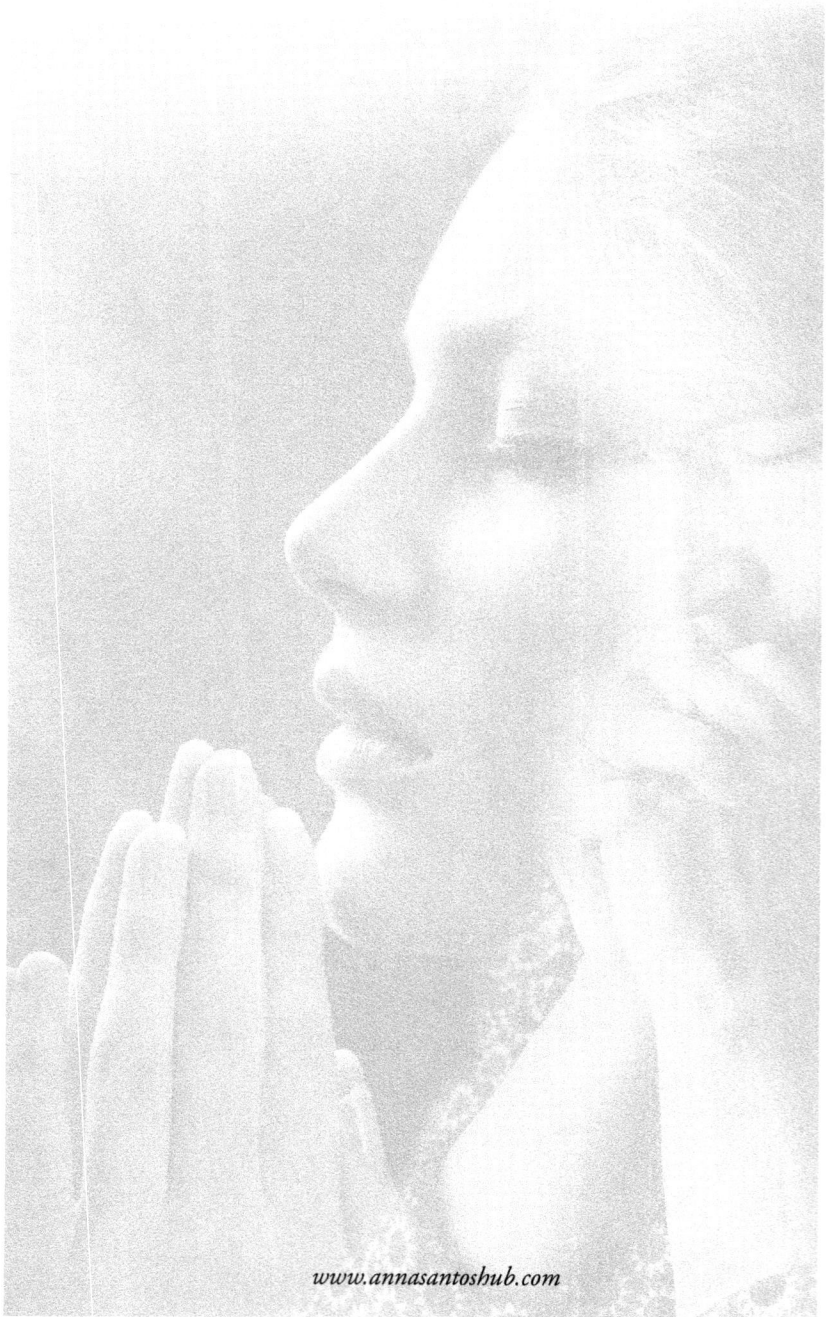

A Woman's Amazing *Grays*

How to Age
Gracefully
with a
Life in Sync
with God

Anna Santos

A WOMAN'S AMAZING GRAYS
How to Age Gracefully with a Life in Sync with God

annasantoshub.com

Publisher 10-10-10 Publishing
Markham, ON, Canada
Printed in Canada and the United States of America

DISCLAIMER

This book is presented by the author as informational and inspirational only, and is not intended to manipulate or change other people's religious and spiritual beliefs and practices.

The content is the sole expression and opinion of the author based on her personal experiences and encounters in her own life, utilizing some relevant references and materials to her topic of choice.

The author also acknowledges that this book is NOT an alternative to the use of the Holy Bible to teach the Word of God.

ACKNOWLEDGMENTS

Thank you, **God Almighty,** for loving me despite my limitations and shortcomings, and for revealing Your True Self to me through this book.

To my husband, **Christopher Santos**: thank you for your unwavering love and support. You helped me bring out the best in me. I love you.

To my very precious God-given gifts, my four kids: **Sophia Margarette**, my artist/animator daughter; **Danver Jude**, my musically inclined and talented son; **Santino Miguel**, my engineer-in-the-making son; and **Christiann Mikhail**, my miracle boy. Mom loves you all very much!

To my **parents**, **my siblings**, **relatives**, and **friends** in business, personal, and religious affiliations: thank you very much.

To my birth country, **Philippines**; and to my adoptive country, **Canada**: thank you for giving me two places to call home.

Special thanks to **Bro. Don Quilao** and **Fr. Kenneth Lao** for your spiritual guidance and support.

Last but not least, my life has significantly changed because of my role model, my inspiration, my God-sent angel, **Bro.**

Bo Sanchez.   I'd always be grateful for the huge impact you've contributed to my life, which I'm now teaching others, too. Thank you so, so much.

And to all of you, **my readers** and **followers** globally: thank you very much.

Accept God's abundant blessings such that you can share them as well to others.

Anna Santos
Serial Mommy Entrepreneur
Author, Certified Life Coach, Speaker

TABLE OF CONTENTS

INTRODUCTION

"Do not complain about growing old.
It is a privilege denied to many."
– Mark Twain

It was during the wee hours of a Saturday morning when…

"My Gosh!!!

"Hon, look at this… see! See it closely!"

"What?"

While cramming in front of the mirror, I exclaimed, "I have gray hair showing, seriously?! Noooooooooooooo…"

My first thought was, "I'm not just thinking old, because I'm literally getting old."

I went back to our bedroom and sat down in deep reflection about my life, asking myself, "Anna, where are you now? You're getting old by the day. You can't stop the clock from ticking!"

Meanwhile, the mini-torture I inflicted on myself suddenly shifted into something positive in my head.

I'm in my mid-forties at the time of this writing. I know; I'm still too young for many. I felt grateful for having reached this age, alive and well, because I also know that there is a surefire death count in the world today, every second. I hope and pray that I can still reach fifty, seventy-five, or even hundred years old, and age gracefully as I collect gray hair and live my one precious life in sync with God.

And speaking about God, I have a confession to make.

Due to overabundance of religious and spiritual teachings these days, the Word of God is, for the most part, taken out of context—thus, the intentional message is changed by addition and/or deletion, leading to varying interpretations of some lines in the scripture.

I don't know about you, but, at some point, I become confused, too. And through prayer, deep reflection and discernment, spiritual counselling, and further research, I'm led back to the journey where God wants me to go—a life in sync with Him.

I have to warn you, though. I'm not a theologian or a Bible expert. I'm an ordinary woman, a wife, and a mom. And like everyone else, I'm a sinner—maybe worse off than most of you. But the good news is, God is not done with you and me yet. We're still a work-in-progress.

As Christians, we're all called to the path towards holiness, to sainthood. Though it may sound intimidating, there's a way. Jesus showed the way.

For all we know, saints were also ordinary people like you and me, who had their respective setbacks, but they followed Jesus. However, following Him isn't easy, as substantiated by the stories of Jesus's twelve apostles, among others, some two thousand years ago.

Now, the question is, "How do we follow Jesus at our present time?"

The world that we now live in has changed the way things work due to natural and man-made events, such as global warming, advanced technology, inventions, and innovations.

As an ordinary woman, I asked God, "How can I follow you, Lord? Everything now seems to be done in a snap! Will my contribution still matter?"

One weekend towards the end of the year 2019, I attended a personal development workshop to prepare myself for the coming new year. A very clear message from the Lord came to me, saying, "*Use your voice. Write a book about me.*"

And I had this inexplicable, lightheaded feeling and chills from my head to the tip of my toes and fingers. It was real; I felt it! It won't go away.

"I… am to write a book about You? But why me? I don't know a lot about the Holy Bible."

Then, suddenly, Mama Mary's image vividly came across my mind.

And I thought, "Do I need to pray Hail Mary now?"

"No, no… Uhm… Oh, yeah."

"Oh, yes, Mary said a resounding YES to You. Christmas, right?"

"Okay, Lord. I'm in. I'm writing a book about you. But, please, help me. I'm not good at this."

So, what now? What's my title? What do I write about You?

"Be still and know that I'm God." – Psalm 46:10

I discerned, asked for His leading through the Holy Spirit. And I looked at myself in the mirror.

Oh, wow, now, I get it! I'm sharing my life through this book and how God worked and continues to work in me.

Done deal.

My life is very, very far from perfect. It's a consistent struggle every single day for me. But, I know, there's a way; I told you.

Now, a woman with gray hair is writing a book about having a life in sync with God. Aha! That's my book title!

Guided by the Holy Spirit, we have to follow Jesus. In other words, be **SPIRITUAL UNDER THE SON.**

Let me explain briefly.

The word "**S-P-I-R-I-T-U-A-L**" was chunked down to actionable steps, as follows:

> **S** – Surrender
> **P** – Pray
> **I** – Imitate
> **R** – Resurrect
> **I** – Intercede
> **T** – Trust
> **U** – Understand
> **A** – Act
> **L** – Love

Under the Son means being a follower of Jesus, the Son of Man, through His perfect examples.

This book is not just for you. Although I'm its author, it's for me, too, to read, apply, and remind myself all the time. In fact, while writing this book, I was tested, hit my rock bottom, and was in the brink of not pursuing it. But God revealed His True Self to me.

And I'm excited to share that with you.

So, let's get started.

CHAPTER 1

SURRENDER

"I can do all things through Christ who strengthens me."
– Philippians 4:13

Nobody is spared from experiencing challenges and problems and chaos in this journey called life. When it seems no longer bearable, our human nature is to give up.

When I became a mother, my story changed. Giving up is no longer an option, because I know I have more reasons to continue now than before. But I would still have moments of wanting to throw in the towel. That's my truth.

Generally speaking, we often associate giving up with surrendering; however, I realized these are two different things.

There seems to be a sense of failure attached to giving up, as though there's no more resolution to make things work. Our body, mind, and spirit just want to shut down, screaming, "I can't take this anymore!!! I'm done."

However, I found a better way to deal with my troubles than giving up—and that is to surrender. This creates a better sense of space and peace of mind for me, even just for a moment. Through this, I'm able to acknowledge that there are things I can't do alone; I need help.

To surrender means to let go and allow that feeling of space, peace, and calmness to flow over to a supernatural being.

I cast my concerns and worries to God—my lifeline.

"I did my best, Lord. It's your turn now. From where I stand, I surrender."

WHY WE ALWAYS FAIL

Failure is inevitable. There's no crystal ball to say with certainty what's going to happen a minute from now. As any successful people honestly admit, they fail from time to time; the difference between them and the rest of the world is how they handle their failures. They use them to become the better versions of themselves.

No one is spared from experiencing failures, and I've had a fair share of them. That's really happening in our physical world.

The History of the Past

The creation of the universe, written in the book of Genesis, is the history of the past.

On the sixth day of creation, according to the scripture, man was created. And here it goes:

"Then God said, "Let us make humankind in our image, according to our likeness; and let them have dominion over the fish of the sea, and over the birds of the air, and over the cattle, and over all wild animals of the earth, and over every creeping thing that creeps upon the earth. So, God created humankind in His image, in the image of God he created them; male and female he created them." – Genesis 1:26-27

It was a beautiful imagery to live in the entire planet with everything on it for the first couple—Adam and Eve—to consume and enjoy that could be passed on to their offspring(s); a perfect condition with a perfect life in a perfect place—so-called paradise.

But something went wrong.

"The Lord God took the man and put him in the garden of Eden to till it and keep it. And the Lord God commanded the man, 'You may freely eat of every tree of the garden; but of the tree of the knowledge of good and evil you shall not eat, for in the day that you eat of it, you shall die.'" – Genesis 2:15-17

They were provided with all they needed; however, God gave them one instruction. And failure to follow such would result in an irreparable consequence.

As it turned out, they failed due to disobedience.

This was when the first sin was committed against God, with its corresponding punishment. And the punishment? Suffering and death.

So, how does this disobedience affect us now?

The perfect kind of life—as originally designed by God for the human race—was no longer available to us after disobedience and committing sin. Thus, we will all suffer and die.

"By the sweat of your face you shall eat bread until you return to the ground, for out of it you were taken; you are dust, and to dust you shall return." – Genesis 3:19

In our time today, we are prone to experiencing failures and falling short of enjoying life's fullness and perfection as part of God's original purpose for us, because sin destroyed it.

Just because each one of us is an heir to Adam and Eve, their original sin crushed God's created harmony for themselves and for all generations after them, including all of us. And now, we experience the effects in our daily life—we suffer; we die.

Through the wickedness of humankind, the harmony of creation was disrupted.

Sin is deceitful, and we must always remember that sinning is a choice in the same way that surrendering to God is also a choice.

When we surrender to God, we reunite with Him by submitting the longings of our hearts such that we become part of the paradise again.

Adam and Eve were given that same choice; they were the first ones to blow it. But here's the thing: you and I aren't cast out from the paradise forever. God invites us back, as He continues to give us a choice every single day—to choose Him.

We've ascertained it from the history of the past. Let's learn from that mistake.

This is His invitation to you and me now. God is always waiting.

Ignoring God's Message and His Messengers

"But they kept mocking the messengers of God, despising his words, and scoffing at his prophets, until the wrath of the Lord against his people became so great that there was no remedy." – 2 Chronicles 36:16

God continuously sends His messengers for years and years until our time now, and, yet, His message is still ignored by many. I'm guilty of that.

Let's go back to Genesis 2:15-17. It was a direct message of God communicated to Adam and Eve, not through a messenger.

But how come it wasn't received well?

"CONTROL."

Humans want control. The enemy (serpent, as described in the Holy Bible) wants to control. We want to step outside of God's control.

I know what you're thinking. I was thinking the same!

Who enticed and tempted Adam and Eve to the forbidden fruit in the first place? The serpent, right?

Although it may seem logical to blame the serpent, it's still Adam and Eve's choice to either obey or disobey God. We know that sinning is a choice, and surrendering to God is a choice as well. There is a consequence for both.

You see, when we do things outside of God's control and we mess up, we blame others—our boss, our co-workers, our neighbors, the economy, the world; we blame God!

That's absolutely me! I play the victim so well, most of the time. When I'd fail to achieve the results I want, I blame my spouse, I blame my surroundings, I blame the internet, I blame everything except ME!

So, then, what are the things that we should surrender to God's control?

Everything. Because to surrender to God literally means to submit to Him all the control. He must take over. He has to be in charge.

But here's the thing: despite God's sovereign power, dominion, and authority over all His creations, He is so compassionate to give us the gift of FREE WILL—choice.

In addition to this gift of choice, humankind is uniquely created in the image and likeness of God (Genesis 1:27), distinct from all other creatures. Humans have mind, body, and spirit.

But what do you do with your mind, with your body, and with your spirit?

There are certain areas in our being that we can and cannot control.

As for me, I know I can control my negative thoughts, my emotions, my belief system, my eating habits, and many other things. I can choose to be motivated or otherwise, and the list goes on.

God has always the last say. And that's the part we cannot control.

Despite our shortcomings, He still wants us to prosper in all areas. Our limitations prevent us from achieving that prosperity, and that's the reason why we need God.

We fail when we do it our way. God has been telling us all along the right way—His way. Our stubbornness blocks His message, and we miss out on that big time.

"From the day that your ancestors came out of the land of Egypt until this day, I have persistently sent all my servants the prophets to them, day after day, yet they did not listen to me, or pay attention, but they stiffed their necks. They did worse than their ancestors did."
– James 7:25-28

We always want to be in charge and in control due to ego and pride.

Being a mom gives me the authority to tell my children what's best for them; however, I've realized that they have their respective individualities and feelings, too. I've ascertained that I should give them supervised independence and age-appropriate responsibilities to discover themselves.

Surrendering control is a reflection of one's character— humility.

In my search to suffice my limited understanding about God, I asked one of my spiritual advisors this question: "What do we really need to give God, because He owns everything?"

I was blown away by the answer; "*No. He doesn't have everything. He doesn't have your sins. He also doesn't have your anger, your unforgiveness, your frustration, your worries, your confusion, your doubts, your guilt, your fear. He doesn't have the whole YOU yet. Surrender everything to Him.*"

My jaw dropped, as my tears fell down like a river flowing in a stream. I was immensely hit; I couldn't move and speak.

It was revealing, indeed. God spoke straight to my heart. The message was flawless.

My friend, God is waiting for you. He wants to connect with you in a very special way. Invite Him and say, "Here I am, Lord. Your servant is listening."

Wrong Association and Crowd

In the business arena, Jim Rohn, an author, motivational speaker, and entrepreneur said, "You're the average of the five people you spend the most time with."

Whether we like it or not, we are influenced by the company we keep. It affects, both positively and negatively, our belief systems, decision-making, values, practices, and even our morality. The scripture offers advice on what to do when these situations arise.

In the Holy Bible, King Solomon had this problem, which can be yours and my problem, too. He was the third and last king in the ancient United Kingdom of Israel, the second son of King David (the father) and Bathsheba (the mother). When his father died, Solomon resumed his father's kingship.

King Solomon received a divine gift from God. Because he was doing so well, God was impressed and King Solomon had found favor with Him. He was celebrated for his knowledge and wisdom, riches and wealth, and honor. However, he succumbed to the temptations of lesser men that led him to sinful acts of lust, ungratefulness, disloyal actions and attitude, which provoked the anger and judgment of God.

"Do not be deceived. Bad company ruins good morals." – 1 Corinthians 15:33

Social media is very beneficial these days—primarily for connections—but it also can be an open door to trigger peer pressure, resulting in associating ourselves with the wrong crowd.

My finances were in a total mess in 2006 until I joined the Truly Rich Club in 2010, led by Bro. Bo Sanchez. My money habits significantly improved, and I became a financial literacy advocate. My advocacy grew to help others as well, and I became a licensed financial adviser in Ontario, Canada, from 2010 until 2017.

I consciously changed for the better in many areas of my life, because I chose to associate myself with the right crowd.

The Demands of Life

"Hon, can I buy a new purse? I need a new one now. By the way, Michael Kors is on sale. It's a good deal. Can I?"

"Hon, can I buy a Louis Vuitton purse? Because the one that I bought last time is now worn out and I need it for work. By the way, Louis Vuitton is on sale. It's a good deal. Can I?"

I'm stopping right here. Because there's more, or it would be an endless list.

Here's my point: we're distracted by the demands of life. I was guilty of "keeping up with the Joneses".

I immigrated to Canada with my family in the mid-2000s. I fortunately landed a good-paying job. Money was easily accessible. I had many credit cards and became hooked. I indulged myself in wasteful shopping sprees. Materialism consumed me. I drowned in huge, bad debt. Thanks to Bro. Bo Sanchez for a 180-degree turn of events in my life, especially financially and spiritually.

I surrendered my shopping addiction, and God healed me.

I now spend my money on things that matter to me, such as God's works, my relationships, travel, self-development, and other healthier endeavors.

Giving in to the demands of life brings confusion rather than satisfaction. Because of that, we're missing out on the opportunity to focus on our true purpose, which I will discuss later.

It also creates frustration when we don't get the things we want, and we end up feeling restless, exhausted, and depressed.

Complacency

"I know your works; you are neither cold nor hot. I wish that you were either cold or hot." - Revelation 3:15

What is complacency?

According to Cambridge Dictionary, "It is a feeling of calm satisfaction with your own abilities or situation that prevents you from trying harder."

So, then, a person who displays this trait is complacent or is better described as apathetic—somebody who has the absence of interest in or concern about life and everything in it.

At some point in our lives, we experience complacency or apathy. I have my own seasons, too! The problem with that is, when it becomes our way of life, excuses bombard us and we miss out on the opportunity to grow more. When things don't turn out the way we plan them to be, we simply accept things as they are, as we comfortably say, "I'm okay. I'm good."

When we deny ourselves of becoming more, we're also preventing to share more—sad, but true. As the saying goes, "We can't pour from an empty cup."

In other words, if we remain complacent, we stall our growth. And the scripture made it clear that when you're not growing, you're dying. Because if that's the case, you're in danger. I'm in danger.

As a Christian, contentment in Christ is to be celebrated, which is a good thing. However, complacency in Christ promotes a false sense of security that creates a lukewarm faith by a complacent Christian, which is one of the greatest dangers in the Christian life.

We are faced with different battles every single day. When we try to solely rely on our own limited strengths and capabilities, we'll surely end up on the losing end of the thread. Christ is our stronghold that never gives way until the battle is won.

I suffered from Postpartum Depression after giving birth to my fourth child, sometime in 2012.

One day, I found myself scribbling in my laptop. As tears fell down my cheeks, free-flowing texts populated my blank

Word document. It continued for several weeks—no editing or proofreading whatsoever.

To cut the story short, I was able to self-publish my first book online in 2012, and the rest is history. Had I succumbed to the depression I felt back then, I won't be the person that I am now.

I refused to be complacent; instead, I chose to receive the grace of God. I let Him use me for His glory. And this book is another example, which at the time of this writing is my fourth one as a solo author and my seventh one with co-authors.

We also exhibit complacency when we don't strive to reach our maximum potential by using the talents and gifts that God gave us, as well as the resources available to us, for His glory. Why? It's probably because of this one dogmatic expression that when we have ambitions towards success, it's ungodly. In effect, most of us tend to just stay where we are, or else we're sinning against God. But here's the bigger problem: staying stagnant invites procrastination, idleness, and then laziness.

"The hand of the diligent will rule, while the lazy will be put to forced labour." – Proverbs 12:24

And this is why we need to seek God's will. We fail because we do things on our own.

I actually didn't intend to become an author—not in my wildest dreams. What I really wanted back then was to become a medical doctor and/or a journalist, but God allowed that I experience a painful stage in my life so that His true purpose for my existence is realized.

Be honest here for a second when I ask you, "Do you like reading a messy book?"

Of course, not! I'm not saying that my book is perfect. It can never be 100% error-free; I know that.

My point is this: I continuously invest in myself—in my writing, speaking and communicating, and in other areas, so that God can use me more effectively to bless others. Because of that, I can't remain complacent; I want to give my best for God's glory as my form of worship.

If singing is your gift, enroll in voice lessons and improve it. Do you love baking? Learn more about it, so you can create an income to feed your family, or teach others to do the same. It can be anything.

Everyone is born unique with talents to share. The world needs you.

SPIRITUAL DRYNESS

"Let anyone who is thirsty come to me and drink." – John 7:37

Dryness or drought. The first thing that comes to my mind is absence of water.

Back in the day, when I was in grade 4, I'd been one of the contenders to represent my school for the track and field competition in the Batangas Region. I had to be physically fit to endure the intense practice day in and day out. However, due to limited food supplies, the only resource that I was pretty sure we never ran out was water.

There were days when our small town would experience a municipality-wide water shortage due to defective pipes. And when that happened, no problem; God would provide rain.

I may not have understood our life's challenges when I was a child; I thought being poor was normal.

What about spiritual dryness? Do we literally drink water to solve it?

You may or you may not be familiar with spiritual dryness, but for the sake of this book, let me share my brief experience with it.

Everyone experiences spiritual dryness in this lifetime; you just didn't realize you've had it. Our faith in God is challenged when troubles come our way, as though He has abandoned us. You then end up feeling isolated and losing interest and motivation in life.

I started to serve a religious group when I was fourteen years old through the music ministry. We'd practice twice weekly. Although I was financially limited at that time, I'd never been absent.

Until, I experienced a major life's crisis in my mid-twenties. I withdrew myself from the group. My personal connection with God also declined. "Whatever" became my favorite word. I totally lost interest in everything. Although I was financially limited at that time, I'd never been absent until I experienced a major life's crisis in my mid-twenties.

How did I get past that?

I surrendered and went back home to God.

The Burden of Guilt

"Everyone who commits sin is guilty of lawlessness; sin is lawlessness." – 1 John 3:4

From the Holy Bible, we know that the fall of man started when Adam and Eve disobeyed God, resulting in committing the original sin.

We also know now that committing sin is a choice, and that a choice leads to a definite consequence.

We learned it from their mistake.

When we sin, it means that we break our relationship with God and our fellowmen as a consequence of our wrongdoings, wickedness, and transgressions that are not in harmony with God's laws and standards. Subsequently, we feel the burden of guilt.

Years ago, I had a friend from a different religious group, who happened to be one of its leaders. She was very active and dedicated in her service. She was full of energy, and her mere presence would make you feel already blessed. We both became busy and never had the chance to talk again.

Many years had passed and I learned from a mutual friend that she resigned from her ministry work. Fortunately, I was able to get hold of her and had the opportunity to talk. She admitted to me her reason of leaving her post—adultery. She had a sexual relationship with a married man.

"I know that God is mad at me. I sinned. I don't deserve to be in the group anymore. I'm bad. I'm ashamed," she uttered in a gargling voice.

Guilt and shame ate her up. Although I couldn't condone the sin, I reassured her that God is merciful and He is a God of second chances.

"*Therefore, if anyone is in Christ, the new creation has come. The old one has gone, the new is here!*" – 2 Corinthians 5:17

When we're spiritually weak, we can easily give in to the temptations around us that will result in committing sin. And when we sin, we develop guilt that separates us from God.

It's the spiritual warfare that we suffer from all the time, which is a lie that condemns us with thoughts like, "God is angry with me." "I don't think I belong to God's kingdom." "I'm sinful, and I don't deserve God's love."

We all have sinned, and we continue to sin due to our human condition and nature. And you may have experienced being judged by others, with their verdict on you as being "guilty".

Dismiss the thoughts that God is punishing you because you've sinned. Sin—in and of itself—is already a punishment.

And don't forget this absolute truth:

"Jesus died for your sins and my sins. He paid our penalty in full."

But remember this: just because He already won the battle for us doesn't mean we can commit sin over and over again. That's a different discussion, which I'll tell you more about in the next pages.

My point is this: the feeling of guilt is a lie—a lie that separates us from God. When you fall, get up, and do better next time, in the same way that Jesus told Mary Magdalene to sin no more when she was in the verge of being stoned to death as punishment for committing adultery.

Harboring that ugly feeling takes us away from the truth—that despite our sinfulness, we are God's children.

And talking about children, I'm a mom to four young kids. I am their first teacher, and it's my duty to maintain my household as their safest haven to learn and grow as God-fearing human beings.

However, when a truckload of tasks takes its toll on me, my patience as a mom is challenged, leaving me angry and frustrated most of the time. When my children commit mistakes and house rules are violated, their guilt feelings show up in different ways— silence, crying spells, and tantrums, to cover up and cope.

If you're a parent like me, you can surely picture what patience looks like and up to what extent of tolerance you can bear for the sake of love.

How much more with our God? He gave His life for you and me. What else can He not do?

God awaits you to go back to His home where you belong, just like in the story of the Parable of the Prodigal Son, found in Luke 15:11-32.

You're lost and now you're found.

Overcoming Pains

"Jesus answered, 'Those who are well have no need of a physician, but those who are sick; I have come to call not the righteous but sinners to repentance.'" – Luke 5:31-32

I have been suffering from vertigo since I was a teenager. Vertigo attacks me randomly without a warning. And when it does, it's such an extremely uncomfortable physical condition to bear.

When there's pain, we seek healing.

While we experience physical pain, there's also emotional pain. We are hurt when we feel violated, cheated on, lied to, betrayed, and taken advantage of. The difference is, we don't seek healing at once when we experience emotional pain, because our tendency is to retaliate, right? That's is very human.

I, for sure, would think about vengeance. Remember, hurt people hurt people.

Many years ago, I was in dire need of funds. Somebody close to me offered her help, and I trusted her intention. I was really thankful to her and expressed my gratitude to the best of my abilities. I paid the debt in full and moved on. After some time, I received a phone call, and she asked for monetary help. Despite being broke due to huge debt at that time, I was able to lend a portion of the money she needed. She didn't receive it well, which started her rage against me. I tried several times to reconcile, but unforgiveness ate her up. I'd hear bad things she'd say about me, so I chose to love her from a distance.

Forgiveness, in and of itself, is God's grace that heals even the deepest wound, which, we, humans can't give on our own.

Because of the fall of man, we suffer from pain and death as the consequence. But, through God's goodness and mercy, we're invited to experience life's fullness and eternity in His kingdom again.

To heal every kind of pain, we must consult the greatest physician and healer of all, because even without opening our lips, He already knows exactly what we need.

Fellowship

"No man is an island."

It's an old adage known to many, which simply means that everyone relies on the company of others in order to live and thrive.

Human beings are naturally social. Even if you believe that you're the most reserved and timid person on the face of the earth, I bet you still feel the need to have at least someone to get along with.

When spiritual dryness attacks you, fellowship with other believers is one of the best ways to overcome it. You're comforted to know that somebody is there to console you and pray for you when you most need it.

The same holds true for other issues we experience in our life— be it addiction, feelings of isolation, depression, and so on. The primary purpose of being in a fellowship, religious or not, is for faster recovery, as it's a form of social support that promotes a sense of belongingness to restore a broken person.

Since we know how a fellowship is done by and for humans, the question now is this: How can fellowship be experienced with God whom we don't see and touch?

A sensible question, isn't it?

We know that human fellowship with God first occurred when Adam and Eve were given instructions over the dominion of all His creations in the Garden of Eden. However, their communion with God was broken after their disobedience, leading to their exile from paradise.

Since then, sin separated humans from God, which continues to be the case today due to our wickedness and wrongdoings. But because of God's goodness and mercy, He offers us His unwavering invitation to partake of His divine nature, including the capacity to love, do good deeds, forgive, become merciful and patient, exercise gentleness and kindness, etc.

"We proclaim to you what we have seen and heard, so that you also may have fellowship with us. And our fellowship is with the Father and with His son, Jesus Christ." – 1 John 1:3

Fellowship with God is at the very heart of what it means to be a follower of Christ —being a Christian, so to speak. Christianity is not just about observance of traditions or laws but rather a personal relationship with the Living God. And for a fellowship to happen, there must be harmony and congruency above everything else.

So, how can we really have a fellowship with Him?

It's by knowing God and His absolute holiness—the divine nature of Him who's seated on the highest throne—first. Second, we should walk in the light of Jesus, refusing sin. We are also in fellowship with God when we confess our sins, so that we can experience His forgiveness, cleansing, and healing.

The Catholic church considers the Holy Mass as the highest and the most beautiful form of worship. The Holy Mass is divided into two main parts: The Liturgy of the Word and the Liturgy of the Holy Eucharist; the latter is the part where Jesus Christ is really, truly, and substantially present in the consecration of the bread and wine, becoming His true body and blood. In our time today, charismatics call the Holy Mass as "breaking of the bread" to signify Jesus's breaking bread and partaking of it among His disciples during the Last Supper before His death. Anthropologists call this commensality, which literally means "table fellowship or the act of eating together in one table".

My husband and I attend a small gathering for married couples to help us grow in our relationship with each other and with God. We have counselling about family and parenting, Bible study, and sharing and reflection. The group calls it "fellowship".

We also have different fellowships in our parish for children of all ages, youths, singles, handmaids, and seniors.

Whatever the case may be, everyone needs somebody to experience and share the love of Christ, whether you're a believer or not.

Receiving God's Gift

A gift is a symbolism that we give and receive for special occasions like Christmas, birthdays, anniversaries, achievements, promotions, and so on.

Regardless of religious beliefs, the Christian roots of gift-giving must have originated from the story of the nativity or the birth of Jesus Christ when the three wise men offered precious gifts to symbolize His royalty and kingship.

Although nobody in our generation today has ever personally witnessed this—the greatest story ever told in human history—it was written in the Gospel of John.

"And the Word became flesh and lived among us, and we have seen his glory, the glory as of a father's only son, full of grace and truth." – John 1:14

What a beautiful gift there is!

As Christians, we profess our faith by saying, "In the Name of the Father, and of the Son, and of the Holy Spirit," which means that the faith of all Christians rests on the Holy Trinity. In the Christian doctrine of the Holy Trinity, we worship God through Jesus Christ in the Holy Spirit. And the mystery of the Most Holy Trinity is the central mystery of Christian faith and way of living, which is the mystery of God in Himself.

During the nativity, the Father was revealed by the Son, Jesus Christ. When we receive the Son, we receive the Father as well, and then the Father and the Son are revealed by the Holy Spirit.

I used to get confused when I was younger as to whether we have three Gods, until I learned about the Holy Trinity as One God in three persons, also called the "Consubstantial Trinity," which means that the divine persons do not share the one divinity among themselves, but each one of them is God whole and entire.

I attended my first *Catholic Life in the Spirit Seminar* in Quezon City, Philippines, in October 1991. It was when I had actually experienced a personal encounter with God, particularly during the Receiving God's Gift part, where I was baptized in the Holy Spirit.

During our speaker's talk, he described the Pentecost that happened several days after the resurrection of Jesus Christ where the Holy Spirit descended upon His followers and spoke in tongues.

In our time today, we receive the same Holy Spirit at baptism, making us adopted sons and daughters of God.

Since being a renewed Christian in 1991, I've developed my personal relationship with God. Although temptations still linger, I'm reassured that the Holy Spirit guides me all the time.

> *"Come, Holy Spirit, I need you*
> *Come, sweet Spirit, I pray*
> *Come in your strength and your power*
> *Come in your own gentle way."*

Do you want a gift that never expires?

Surrender your worries by calling upon the Holy Spirit for the renewal of your soul.

The Heart of Worship

"My sheep hear my voice. I know them, and they follow me." – John 10:27

Have you reached the point where you thought God has abandoned you, because your prayers are still left unanswered?

Many times, I'd feel the same, as though God is ignoring me, until I realized in my deep contemplation that it's actually the other way around; it's I who ignore God all these years. I dismiss the fact that He has been there all along, calling me, but due to the noise of the world, I couldn't hear His voice.

We live in an era where everything is made available online. We have unlimited access to all the information and things we need in a matter of a few seconds and clicks. Communication is made easy by the day through the innovative inventions that are readily accessible by many. Advanced technology has disrupted people's ability to walk, talk, think, and act, as poor Siri and Alexa became the household alternatives to do these tasks for humans.

Gadgets distract almost everyone, resulting in accidents and road rage; they sabotage children's natural brain development and physical health, compromise quality family time and bonding to improve relationships, and the list goes on. These are not bad things, except when they are misused and overused.

The real spiritual worship starts from the heart, delighting in Jesus to express our praises and gratitude for what He had done for us. Worship is all about focusing our comforted heart to Jesus, putting our trust and confidence in the Risen Lord.

In the Parable of the Lost Sheep, the scripture created a very vivid imagery of God's love for us—in that whenever you and I go astray, He leaves the rest of the herd to find and bring us back to His flock where we truly belong.

It was sometime in July 2006 when my second child, who was then in Junior Kindergarten, was left in the care of a trusted friend because my work was almost two hours away from where we used to live. I requested this friend of mine to pick up my son from school that day. I was on the subway on my way home when I suddenly received a phone call. To my horror, it was my friend, telling me that my son was nowhere to be found at school. My anxiety escalated even more when the school confirmed to me that my son was really missing.

I felt extremely anxious and scared. As soon as I got off the train, I ran as fast as I could to catch another bus going to the school. Bewildered and worried, I almost got hit by a car, but I didn't care, because I wanted to find my son. I called my neighbor to look after my other child while finding my lost son. After roughly an hour, we learned that he boarded the wrong school bus. Praise God, my son was back! It was one of the scariest but happiest days of my life.

You can surely imagine how it was for a mom like myself to have reunited with her lost child. God is more than that. He never stops from pursuing you and me. He paid the highest cost for us to reunite with Him and be part again of His home.

Surrender to His love. It's the most secure spot you can find.

FINDING REST

"Our heart is restless until it rests in God." – St. Augustine

Have you ever wondered why, at times, you feel restless in many aspects?

In the book of Genesis, God created the universe and everything in it in six days. On the seventh, He rested and contemplated His own work, knowing that it was all good.

The scripture clearly suggests that because God rested, we, too, can rest from work. Believers call it the Sabbath day, which is considered to be sacred.

The demands of life point us to become focused more on making money, but please don't get me wrong here. I'm not saying that making money is bad at all. I believe it only becomes a problem when our intentions are not aligned with God's will and purpose.

Although I can't really judge people, because I don't know their situation, many here in Canada have two, three, and even four jobs. Our physical bodies can only take as much work, and pushing our limits will surely make us feel restless.

When irresponsible spending due to materialism consumed me many years ago, I justified my long working hours to pay the bills, sacrificing my quality time with myself and my family. I almost wrecked our marriage, let alone my own sanity.

Machines become tired, too. And when they do, they fail to function well. Just like us, human beings, when we feel drained, exhausted, and burnt out—we fail to function well and serve our true purpose.

But let me point this out: to rest doesn't mean to be complacent. Resting requires a temporary removal of oneself from the usual labor or work for a living to focus on what's more important.

Claiming God's Word

"The grass withers, the flower fades; but the word of our God will stand forever." – Isaiah 40:8

In this fast-paced, ever-changing world where promises are usually broken, it becomes harder to trust. Because of that, most of us put little to no value at all on words—spoken or written.

Before becoming a stay-at-home mom and an online business owner, I'd usually spend sixteen hours almost every day working, as I had my full-time job in the hospital on top of my several side hustles. I had a very frantic schedule, and coffee became my constant companion to fill me up.

I'd seldom see my children due to work deadlines.

One evening, my third child, who was five years old at that time, asked me if we could go to the park to play, to which I agreed. "Yeah, sure. This coming weekend, baby."

That weekend came, and he said, "Mommy, let's go to the park."

"No, we can't. Not today, please. Mommy is busy. Next Saturday, promise."

As expected, we didn't go that following Saturday.

He was only five years old, and I thought he'd forget about it.

Two years later, he randomly mentioned it in our casual conversation, "Mommy, you didn't take me to the park."

Ouch. I felt ashamed, because I know I hurt my son. He held on to my promise, but I failed him.

Lesson learned: broken promises hurt feelings, and the main casualties are mostly the people we love.

But God is not like that. Because of His great love for us, He's faithful and keeps His Word. He's the same God yesterday, today, and forever.

It's such a relief to know that, when life gets tough and answers are nowhere to be found, I can find rest in God and His Word.

"And we know that all things work together for good for those who Love God, who are called according to his purpose." – Romans 8:28

This became my anchor to continue with life regardless of the circumstance. He promised that all things—victories and wins and persecution and sufferings—will be for my best interest.

Because we're all children of God, it's music to His ears to ask for anything and claim His Word.

Being Still

"Be still, and know that I am God! I am exalted in the earth." – Psalms 46:10

Be Still
By Hillsong

"Hide me now
Under your wings,
Cover me
Within your mighty hand,

When the oceans rise and thunders roar
I will soar with you above the storm
Father, You are King over the flood
I will be still and know You are God

Find rest my soul
In Christ alone,
Know His power
In quietness and trust."

I only had $100.00 left in my wallet, but I gave it to my needy, older brother the morning of my third day in the Neuro-Linguistic Programming (NLP) certification workshop that I attended sometime in the spring of 2018 in Toronto, Canada. Because I'd allocate our weekly funds, that $100.00 was not an extra money for me to begin with.

In the said workshop, there were exercises that required our participation. We were fifty-plus in the room. As I was seated at the very front row, the facilitator called me, and, so, I stood up.

My part would be to answer some questions. He then handed me a $100.00 as a prop —yes, a prop. We finished the exercises and as I was about to hand back the bill to the facilitator, he held my hand and said, "It's yours."

"What? Mine! Really?"

I became teary-eyed, as I had goosebumps.

I then shared with the whole class about what had happened that morning related to the $100.00 bill.

God reminded me to be still. Worry is not for me to handle but His. Anxiety blocks His power to freely move in us, but once we let go, miracles happen.

"Cast all your anxieties on him, for he cares about you." – 1 Peter 5:7

This may seem petty for you, or you may think it was just a coincidence. But there were different sets of exercises that day without the $100 as a prop. I could have been called to participate earlier or later, or maybe not at all.

I knew God took care of my worry that day. He used the event to fulfill His promise. It also made me realize that He wanted to use me as His instrument of love, hope, and provision. God requires our participation for miracles to happen in other people's lives.

You may be in a more difficult situation right now where worrying is the only thing you can do. But let me ask you this: Does that help you to make things any better?

When the Lord said to us that we be still and know that He is God, He didn't actually say that it's wrong to worry or feel anxious. He's just reminding us that there's a better alternative—in that we don't have to bear the ugly feeling. We can cast our worries and surrender everything to Him, because He is bigger than whatever challenges we face.

We are, in fact, encouraged to stop wrestling with the battles that are not ours to fight in the first place. He's in full control.

Being a Good Listener

They say that mothers know best.

I was a daughter first before I became a mom. Because of that, I believe there's a better way to translate the line above.

I'm 100% sure that every mother in the world always wants the best for her children. However, it doesn't mean that she always knows what's best for them.

I was brought up differently compared to how I raise my own children now, probably due to primitive cultural practices, values, and parenting styles. Back in the day, I wasn't allowed to freely state my feelings, or it would be regarded as being disrespectful.

I always make it clear to my children now that I'm here to guide and support them, but they're the ones who'll make a decision for themselves, especially when it's time to do so. I gave them the opportunity to speak up and share their point with respect, if needed.

I was in university when my friends planned a field trip, about two hours away from the city. Initially, my mother did not give me permission to go, but upon my persistence, I was finally given the green light. I packed my things and as I headed to our meeting place, I felt anxious. When we were about to leave, I asked the driver of our service car to open the door because I needed to get off. At that point, a sense of discomfort overcame me. Although my mother allowed me to go, she made a comment to have caused that strange feeling inside of me—something about listening to the gut feeling, which her mother (my maternal grandmother) taught her.

To cut a long story short, a car accident happened during that trip. Fortunately, nobody died, but some of my friends sustained non-life-threatening injuries. I could have been part of that traumatic experience had I not listened to my mother. The incident served a very important lesson that I still carry with me today.

I'd become better at following and listening, especially to those who have my best interest at heart—my mother is one of them.

When we're exposed to an imminent danger, God talks to us in different ways through people, events, circumstances, nature, music, or even a random text in a book or in an advert.

We oftentimes miss out on God's distinct message when we chose being reactive over being responsive.

I learned from my life coaching certification program that—to be an effective life coach—I must be very, very good at listening to my clients. Because the reality is, poor listening diminishes the other person, while good listening displays an act of compassion or empathy. I realized that life coaching is not just a profession but ministry work as well. Good listening skills enable me to ask perceptive questions, so that I can prepare myself to respond appropriately after the whole story has been heard from a nonjudgmental stance.

As a mother to four—two teenagers and two toddlers, at the time of this writing—I have to adjust my listening skills, because they have unique needs. Listening to their concerns every single day, although it may seem exhausting, is a gift. Oh, I almost forgot. I have a husband who has his concerns, too! So, I have five to deal with ☺.

Dealing with five different personalities in my household 24/7 is actually a very good training ground that I can apply to help me become a more effective life coach to my students.

Exercising Humility

"*Hey, I love your purse. It looks really nice.*" The lady on the subway commented.

I responded by saying, "*Oh, it's very cheap.*"

Sometimes, being humble is taken out of context. I used to define humility as something else. I could have just said "thank you" to her. No explanations or justifications needed.

Many of us have the wrong understanding as to what true humility means in the Holy Bible.

More often than not, when we say we are not good, we are humble. It's not the case.

Godly humility is being comfortable with who you are in the Lord, recognizing that we need God's help to accomplish things in our lives, including our personal goals and dreams. And when these are accomplished, we are readily able to give credit to the Main Source and that our accomplishments are not from our own doing and strength, but God's.

True humility also requires being free from pride and arrogance. Sometimes, it's okay to defend our own points of view, but winning the argument shouldn't be the goal when a certain situation arises. God is teaching us to resolve conflicts by exercising gentleness and humility.

"A soft answer turns away wrath, but a harsh word stirs up anger."
– Proverbs 15:1

Jesus Christ is the perfect example of humility, and we are called to exercise the same. Despite His divine nature, He stooped down to our level and lived as a human being.

Raising teenagers requires a lot of patience and humility. Their fluctuating moods would just blow up randomly and test my patience. I've come to some moments where I'd shout at them, as I felt it wasn't fair being disrespected. I'm their mother, right? However, it takes God's grace and mercy to collect my composure and courage to say, "I'm sorry" to my children, when needed.

I grew up in a culture where parents didn't really apologize to their children, even when it was obviously their fault. It must have been their upbringing, too.

I've learned later on in life that being humble doesn't necessarily mean that we stay silent and say nothing; we can state our point without being hostile or aggressive, but rather with compassion and gentleness.

We're aware that every business has a risk. My husband and I invested in real estate rental properties for our four children's future. Being a landlord for more than a decade now has taught me a lot of unprecedented lessons from damaged properties due to both natural and man-made events, to our staff running away with several months' worth of collected rents, to delinquent tenants, and whatnot. I've come to a point of giving up, but God made me realize that these unfavorable events are all a part of it. I've learned how to totally submit to His will to fulfill our purpose, and we can only do that through humility based on Jesus's example.

My experience as a life coach also taught me how to reframe my thoughts to serve me better and be an effective mentor to others.

"But I say to you, 'Do not resist an evildoer. But if anyone strikes you on the right cheek, turn the other also.'" – Matthew 5:39

Steadfastness

"Blessed is anyone who endures temptation. Such a one has stood the test and will receive the crown of life that the Lord has promised to those who love him. – James 1:12

What does steadfast mean?

According to Merriam-Webster Dictionary, it means being firm in belief, determination, or adherence.

In other words, steadfastness requires endurance or tenacity to a certain belief, habit, or simply anything or any person.

For an athlete to be at his best—shape, endurance, performance and stamina—non-negotiable practice is a must.

The same holds true for our faith in God. We'll be tested amidst all forms of afflictions, sufferings, and pains—physical, emotional, mental, and spiritual.

Talking about pain, I was once asked how I could possibly describe childbirth.

And this was my reply: On a pain scale of 1 to 10, 10 being the highest, it's way too low. Because the pain of childbirth transcends more than the physical; there are other aspects associated with it.

I've previously shared my story about Postpartum Depression in 2012. It was an ugly feeling, but I know God allowed that part to give birth to a beautiful story of victory in me. I became a published author of not just one, but seven books now. And I believe I've been called to write more.

The God that we serve is steadfast, and He calls us to be steadfast amidst all trials.

Had I totally given myself in to the nasty feelings of depression and hopelessness during my lowest points, writing this book wouldn't be even possible.

Believe me, it's easier to pray when things are in order—when prayers are answered and when everything is doing well. Christian fortitude requires God's strength in the same way that our cellphones are plugged into the socket to be recharged. It's important that we plug in to the Main Source to ensure that we won't run out of long-lasting battery charge, especially when we need to use our energy. Because here's the thing: when we're running low, our human tendency is to find temporary relief, which can't assure us of a permanent resolution to our problems. God is permanent; the world is temporary.

On my fortieth birthday, sometime in early 2016, we went on a twelve-day Catholic pilgrimage to the Holy Land to seek God's signs. No indications of anything came to me until our last day, when our priest celebrated the Holy Mass at the St. Francis of Assisi. In his homily, he said something along these lines: "*Why are we so worried about retirement that takes us away from what's more important? If you want to love God, love your family first.*"

Wow!

Is God telling me to leave my job that I loved?

I initially felt in denial and couldn't let go.

Two weeks after I returned to Toronto, I came back to work but felt physically sick in that I had to be sent home almost every day, as I couldn't function very well. I had terrible headaches and numbness in my hands. I worked as a medical transcriptionist and transcribing our patients' medical reports was my main duty. I was referred to different specialists, including a neurologist for a brain MRI and a CT scan. Laboratory work was also ordered, but all diagnostic tests came back normal.

Finally, I visited my family doctor for a regular checkup. She was bewildered about my condition, as everything was normal, and she couldn't give me any clear diagnosis. She then asked me a question that shocked me: "Anna, what's bothering you?"

And now, we're talking. A real conversation happened right there and then.

I told her that I went to the Holy Land and shared with her my purpose of the said trip. She advised me to do what my heart tells me.

My brain tells me to stay, but my heart tells me to leave.

And I followed my heart. So, then, I tendered my resignation.

Officially, I became a stay-at-home mom on August 16, 2016. To this day, I enjoy being a full-time mom and a wife.

I shut one door, but God opened more.

I am now coaching other parents and soon-to-be parents, especially moms, about business, self-development, money, and more. I also get invited to speak on stages. And I can truly and strongly feel now that God is up to something great again for me that's aligned with His divine purpose. Let's wait and see.

When I responded to God's calling to take care of His business, He took care of mine.

As the song goes,

> *"Be not afraid. I go before you always.*
> *Come follow me. And I will give you rest."*

THE ART OF LETTING GO

It's our human nature to easily become attached to something or someone, and we sometimes suffer from separation anxiety. As part of our coping mechanism, we tend to look for another means to get past the feeling of longing.

When it was time for our eldest daughter to leave our house and live on her own several hours away to pursue college, it took me a while to accept it.

If you're a mom like myself, you'd understand how it feels—when the time comes that our children have to leave our house to spread their wings, it's painful; however, on the other hand, I've learned that letting go is also an act of love. Although it's emotionally hard, putting the needs of others first above our own is a selfless act, indeed.

So, how do we really let go of any attachments?

We bought a house here in Toronto in 2008, where we lived for roughly ten years. We've had a lot of good memories there, but we decided to sell it and downsize.

My husband was surprised when I suggested selling the house. "Are you serious, hon?" He asked.

Obedience to God is also knowing what matters most.

Although it would be great to stay in the house that I took care of for years, I had to put our daughter's welfare first. She needed the funds for college, and the equity we had accumulated was invested for her three younger siblings.

I love my children more than my house. So, I let go.

Our new house now is way smaller than our previous, but I'm happier. We have more opportunities to bump into each other due to smaller space.

You're Not God

I don't know about you, but I never had any success in trying to boss my children around while trying to teach them to follow me at the same time.

My youngest child was a picky eater. Everyone in my household loves vegetables except him. I'd tried so many tricks, but they all didn't work. He'd really scrutinize everything I served. One day, I thought the trick worked, because he freely put his spoon into his mouth, until he spat the food out. The incident took its toll on me and I shouted at him in frustration. After a while, I talked to him and apologized.

The next day, I again cooked vegetables, but I decided to change my style. During the family conversation, I told my husband to bring me to the eye specialist after lunch due to blurry vision. Then, suddenly, my picky-eater son asked me, "Mommy, are you going to wear glasses?"

"Yes, baby."

"But why?" He asked.

"Well, because I didn't listen to my mommy before. I didn't want to eat healthy foods like vegetables when I was your age. And do you know vegetables are good for the eyes? Like squash, carrots, green leaves…?"

The next day, I didn't cook vegetables.

"Mommy, I want squash," he said.

Thank God. He now eats vegetables—all vegetables.

Here's my lesson learned: "Anna, yes, you are a mom, but you're not God!"

When God wants to teach us something, He does it with love and compassion and not with manipulation.

Anger out of frustration is one letter away from DANGER.

As a mom, there are things I can and cannot control inside my household. The same thing applies as an entrepreneur.

It was such an amazing feeling to have bought our first rental property back in 2009. However, after several months, the feeling of amazement shifted to a huge disappointment when our tenant missed six months' worth of rental payments and damaged our property. Oh, I failed to mention the surmounting stress and sleepless nights associated with that.

Did we stop buying after that incident?

No, we continued instead and, in fact, bought bigger units, because we know challenges won't go away. To this day, we experience bigger problems—from tenants not paying for months, to being scammed, bursting pipes due to extreme cold weather, leaking roofs—you name it. But wait, there's more! You'll find out in the next pages.

Because I acknowledge that I'm limited, I'm letting go and letting God.

Using God's GPS

Global Positioning System, or what we call GPS now, was launched in the United States in the early 1970s for military and navigation purposes. Advanced technology played a huge role in its innovation and easier accessibility for the general public.

Although the traditional maps are still in use even to this day by many for geographical purposes, utilization of modern GPS became prevalent globally by many vehicle owners of all makes and types due to its convenience and more sophisticated features in a matter of a few clicks.

My whole family drove by land to the Disneyland in Orlando, Florida, from Toronto, some years ago. We were almost halfway our roughly 24-hour drive (with rest in between), we felt as though we were driving in circles. We got lost somewhere in Atlanta, Georgia, and wasted an hour or so, leaving us all exhausted and frustrated.

You see, no matter how expensive, sophisticated, or advanced our human GPS system is, glitches can still occur.

I've mentioned early on that my ultimate dream was to become a medical doctor, an idea I bought from my late maternal grandmother.

I took a four-year bachelor's degree program to prepare for medical school. Fast forward, I finished the program but didn't pursue Medicine primarily due to financial difficulties. Years passed, I got married, immigrated to Canada, and continued with my life. I'd been hired by a big hospital in Toronto shortly after landing. One day, I again felt the inclination to pursue medical school. I enrolled in one of the universities in Toronto to pursue it. Two weeks before the school opening, I felt very, very anxious—with feelings of discomfort, emotional disturbance, and crying spells due to unknown reasons. I locked myself up in my bedroom one day and asked for God's wisdom. It dawned on me that it wasn't really my dream but someone else's. I decided to back out.

We should learn again from Adam and Eve when the Lord looked for them, according to Genesis 3:9, where it says:

"But the Lord God called to the man, and said to him, 'Where are you?'"

We know He's God, and we can't hide from Him. But why is He asking Adam and Eve their whereabouts?

God is asking the same question to us today. He wants to know what paths have we taken so far. Have we been following Jesus as the way, the truth, and the life? Are we pursuing His purpose for us?

This is what I know, and I've accepted it along the way.

Because He gave us the gift of free will, He allows us to commit mistakes, so that we can learn from them. But it doesn't mean He abandons us; it's His way of telling us, "I told you so. Here's a better way. My way."

Looking at my life now, I've realized that God has the most precise and error-free navigation. I thank God that I changed my unreliable Global Positioning System and followed His GPS—**God's Positioning System**—instead.

The GPS that we now use is made by humans, which is prone to errors, defects, and miscalculations.

Our life's journey won't be easy. We'd surely have pains in the process, and giving up may seem to be our last resort. In fact, following Jesus doesn't give us the guarantee that our life will be pain-free. It's during our trying times that we know we're not alone, and we don't have to do it on our own.

My prayer changed to something like this: "Lord, don't remove the mountain. Just help me to climb it."

Whenever you feel you've reached the end of the tunnel, remember this:

"It is the Lord who goes before you. He will be with you; he will not fail you or forsake you. Do not fear or be dismayed." – Deuteronomy 31:8

Your Command Center

Our human body is a collection of several systems that work hand-in-hand to function perfectly.

For example, the circulatory system is primarily designed for carrying out the nutrients to other body parts for sustenance. Our reproductive system, obviously, is for propagation of life. Although we know that all our body systems have their respective functions, they have a command center that stands as their big boss where signals are transmitted and being distributed to different body organs.

The human brain—our command center—controls every movement of the human body and its parts. Just the thought of reaching the point that our control source weakens, expires, and dies is really scary.

We, humans, generally speaking, also have a command center whose power is omnipotent and omnipresent. God, as our main command center, never weakens, expires, or dies, which means that we should never be scared.

For my personal development and business endeavours, I hire mentors to tap into their wisdom, because I know I can't grow on my own. I need individuals more experienced, knowledgeable, and credible than myself to teach me how things are done the right way to achieve success—what worked and what didn't.

Asking for help is not a sign of weakness, but rather of courage and of humility. Surrendering pride and ego will take you to the success you've been aiming for much faster.

When you feel that you're not getting anywhere, it's time to acknowledge that you really need help—a reroute.

As Christians, God is our stronghold.

"Oh, the depth of the riches and wisdom and knowledge of God! How unsearchable are His judgments and how inscrutable His ways!" – Romans 11:33

God is pleased when we tap into Him as our main command center without a doubt.

Will you follow Him? No turning back?

The Parable of the Cloth and Wineskins

I teach my life coaching program students how to eliminate their old bad habits and to create new ones that can serve their lives better. This strategy is very familiar to most of us, and, yet, a lot are still not getting it right.

To simplify, we can't expect new results from old habits. That's insane.

Experts say that, for an old habit to be replaced with a new one, a person needs at least twenty-one days to get used to it.

As Christians, we can readily transform our lives when we renounce our sins and become a new creation in Christ.

When I attended the Catholic Life in the Spirit Seminar in 1991 for the first time, it was one of the greatest feelings I've ever experienced. I felt God's invigorating presence in my life, but, shortly thereafter, I regressed to my old ways while professing my renewal. That part of my life reminded me of one of the Parables of the Cloth and Wineskins that says:

"No one sews a piece of unshrunk cloth on an old cloak, for the patch pulls away from the cloak, and a worse tear is made. Neither is new wine put into old wineskins; otherwise, the skins burst, and the wine is spilled, and the skins are destroyed; but new wine is put into fresh wineskins, and so both are preserved." – Matthew 9:16-17

God teaches us that our lives cannot be a combination of two opposite principles. We cannot serve two masters at a time—it's either you're for God, or you're against God. We cannot follow the world and God at the same time.

The new wine represents the truth in God and in His teaching, while the old represents the habits into which we have been born, which we refuse to get rid of, creating prejudice. God's way must completely replace our old and worldly ways, so that we can experience a new life with Jesus. However, when we refuse to have total conversion towards salvation, we burst due to our sinfulness and wicked ways.

If we really want massive changes in our lives, we must acknowledge that we need help and then act on it—as it is for a sick person who seeks a medical doctor's help or for somebody with a dying spirit who needs God for an eternal renewal and spiritual healing.

Unlocking God's Master Plan

When January of the year comes, everyone seems to feel pressured. New Year's resolution becomes the trend, because if you don't have one, you're not in.

Benjamin Franklin once said, "If you fail to plan, you're planning to fail."

As part of our parenting strategy, we have a ten-year-long plan laid out for our children. Is it bad? I don't think so. We're parents, and we just hope for what's best for them.

But here's the truth: no matter how organized our plan is, God always has the last say. And we should hang on to that better plan—God's master plan.

Wouldn't it be nice if God e-mailed us a blueprint of His plan for each one of us? Or maybe an instruction manual from Him attached to our birth certificates when we're born?

Due to overabundance of advices available online and offline, there seems to be an information overload that leads to our confusion. Do I do this, or do I do that? This life proves to be hard and challenging by the day. However, God promises us with a master plan. He wants us to travel light to reach our final destination.

It's very reassuring to hear God say, "I got this, Anna."

"And not only that, but we also boast in our sufferings, knowing that suffering produces endurance, and endurance produces character, and character produces hope, and hope does not disappoint us, because God's love has been poured into our hearts through the Holy Spirit that has been given to us." – Romans 5:3-5

Will you accept God's invitation to unlock His master plan?

INTO THE UNKNOWN

"Have no fear of moving into the unknown."
– Saint John Paul II

One of my greatest fears growing up was being left alone in a dark room. My imagination plays around me, as though a monstrous image would show up any moment before my very eyes. I got past that fear.

The Biggest Risk

I'm a businesswoman, and I know every business has its risks. Investments are the same—you lose or you gain.

One of my mentors said that, in business, it's not losing money that's the biggest risk. He said that what's riskier is not taking risk at all. In other words, doing nothing is risky, and playing safe is just the same.

This idea opened my eyes, and that's how I became a risk-taker in the business realm, but this kind of risk is not really my point here.

While business risk is temporal, we have to be mindful of the biggest risk of all—eternal risk.

This simply means that, when we ignore God's invitation to salvation, we are at risk of losing eternal life.

This reminds me of a conversation between Jesus and a rich, young man in the scripture:

"Jesus said to him, 'If you wish to be perfect, go, sell your possessions, and give the money to the poor, and you will have treasure in heaven; then come, follow me." – Matthew 19:21

We can't really tell when it's our time. Surrendering everything to God is the best thing we can do.

Outside Your Comfort Zone

They say that growth is found outside the comfort zone, and beautiful revelations can come out of a painful experience.

A butterfly is beautiful, but it undergoes a natural process before it becomes one.

As Christians, we are called by God to do the unusual things such as the counter-cultural norms or those that you haven't done before to promote His kingdom.

We're not required to be a priest, a nun, or a preacher/pastor, but if you feel that it's your calling, may God prosper you and bless you more. A random act of kindness to a stranger already counts. Listening to somebody who's hurting also counts. Sharing Jesus and the Good News to others is also a great thing.

You may still not feel ready to step outside your comfort zone. Remember that breakthroughs are not found in ordinary situations. You need to move and face your fears to grow in courage, which God teaches us to do.

When you believe that the Holy Spirit is there readily accessible when you need help, you'll be able to do the things you've never imagined you can do.

Following the Light

"Again, Jesus spoke to them, saying, 'I am the light of the world. Whoever follows me will never walk in darkness but will have the light of life.'" – John 8:12

Power outages were one of the usual challenges in my small hometown back in the day. My grandfather had his way to solve this problem by making an improvised electricity source, called Petromax. It's so bright that its radiance could reach a few blocks more.

On the first day of God's creation of the universe, He said, *"Let there be light"*. Where there's separation between light and darkness—that's our physical light.

Physical light is necessary for human survival; we need sun, for instance.

There's another Light, the Light of Jesus, that we all need for spiritual survival and alignment.

Our life's journey is filled with a lot of uncertainties and challenges, leading us to be tempted to sin over and over again. Following the Light of Jesus is an assurance of salvation that we can enjoy once we come back and reconcile again with God like the prodigal son. God's promise of His light means that there's no need for us to walk again in the darkness of sin and death.

As followers of that One True Light, we are called to be lights for others, so that they can also see that bright light in us, which can be made alive through our good deeds.

We are called to bear witnesses about the Light.

John the Baptist was one of greatest examples written in the Holy Bible, who pointed everybody out to the True Light—Jesus.

"He was a burning and shining lamp, and you were willing to rejoice for a while in his light." – John 5:35

Becoming God's witnesses of the Good News illuminates that light to shine even brighter, so much so when all of us, humans, do it together as one, we can definitely point to that Main Source of brightness that never fades.

We didn't have to suffer like John did during his gruesome death. As ordinary people of today, we can manifest our faith by increasing Christ in us while decreasing ourselves, so that others may see Him more.

May we become God's mouthpiece of truth that our achievements can never be made possible without that One True

Light that we follow. By leading others to go to that same path, we become the bearers of the Good News for the salvation of others as well.

Let's be humble to follow the light, and bring others to the Light of Jesus.

When Fear is Good

Fear is an unpleasant emotion that causes anxiety due to perceived danger or threat.

According to studies, there are two kinds of fears: innate and learned. We're born with only two innate ones—the fear of falling and the fear of loud sounds. And everything else, as one grows older, is acquired and learned that sometimes progresses to phobias.

For the most part, when someone is afraid to explore or do something new due to uncertainties and has a fear of the unknown, his ability to grow is obscured.

Although I've mentioned that fear is an unpleasant emotion, it can be good for us as well. Fear activates our "fight or flight" mechanism to keep us safe and protected from imminent danger, which is the kind of fear that we need in the physical world.

I had the opportunity to speak for twenty minutes and shared the stage with Jack Canfield, the co-creator of the *Chicken Soup for the Soul* series in the past. My topic was about transforming our pains into power to get what we want.

While my sizzle video was being played to introduce me, I walked up the stage and faced the huge crowd. Feeling nervous, I lost my train of thought. I was literally mentally blocked for seconds, not really knowing what to say. I lost everything I prepared for. And the only words I uttered at that very moment were, "Lord, help me. Come, Holy Spirit, I need you."

Then, words suddenly came down to me; I began my speech and finished it flawlessly. I received heartwarming comments from the audience, stating that my message moved them.

Initially, I was hesitant to write this book due to fear; I was afraid of the huge responsibility that goes with it. I don't know a lot of biblical passages to begin with. I'm afraid of detractors. I'm afraid to be persecuted. I'm afraid to be judged. I'm simply afraid.

Fear is good, because it gives us the courage to ask and rely on the greatest provider of all wisdom—God.

"The fear of the Lord is the beginning of wisdom; all those who practice it have a good understanding. His praise endures forever." – Psalm 111:10

When we fear God, it's a very, very positive thing. And when it becomes our lifestyle, it saves us from caving into our own sinful nature. Imagine if all of humankind feared God; people would be more likely to keep their word and treat others with kindness. What a beautiful world it is to live in!

Life can be tough, and facing it alone is scary. However, when we're reassured that we can rely on somebody huge enough to get us covered, our journey feels lighter.

To fear God is an invitation to have room in your life for more of God's love. And we can't make fear go away by sheer force of will, but by an act of surrender, so that we can allow God to pour His love upon us. Allow the Lordship of Jesus to increase such that He can expand in all areas of your life today.

"There's no fear in love, but perfect love casts out fear; for fear has to do with punishment, and whoever fears has not reached perfection in love." – 1 John 4:18

CHAPTER 2

PRAY

"Do not worry about anything, but in everything by prayer and supplication with thanksgiving let your requests be made known to God."
– Philippians 4:6-7

W HY DO WE PRAY AND TO WHOM DO WE PRAY?

God's Word calls us to pray.

Obedience to His will requires us to pray and must be part of our life in Him. Jesus is our role model in living a life of prayer. He, in fact, taught us how to do it through The Lord's Prayer.

Now, you may ask: If Jesus is God, why does He need to pray and to whom does He pray?

The answer is found in understanding the Holy Trinity: one God exists as three persons—the Father, the Son, and the Holy Spirit.

You'll also get the answer by understanding the doctrine of incarnation that Jesus—who is the second person of the Trinity—has two natures: both God and a man, which can be found in John 1:14, *"And the Word became flesh and lived among us, and we have seen his glory, the glory as of a father's only son, full of grace and truth."*

As a man, Jesus needed to pray. When He was praying, He was not praying to Himself, but to God the Father.

Today's Catechism teaches us a very useful framework to remember the key elements when praying such that we can communicate and express ourselves more to God—the ACTS formula—which is the acronym for: A for Adoration, C for Contrition/Confession, T for Thanksgiving, and S for supplication.

Let me discuss each one briefly.

ADORATION

Adoration is a form of prayer to express our highest admiration and reverence, accompanied by worship to acknowledge the presence of the higher being.

As Catholics, we'd normally go to the Blessed Sacrament where the monstrance (a transparent receptable where the consecrated Host is exposed for veneration) is present.

Adoration is a beautiful experience of solitude and calmness while enjoying God's living presence at the same time.

It was in the early 2000s when I felt so confused and helpless and found myself inside the Blessed Sacrament of the EDSA Shrine in Quezon City, Philippines.

With my troubled heart, I couldn't even open my lips to pray. I just sat down at the very back while gazing upon the monstrance. Minutes went by and I felt calmness and peace inside of me. I stayed for two hours and felt like a different person afterwards.

Praise and Worship

To pray is simply a means to communicate with someone deity and sovereign. As Christians, we believe in one God to whom we pray.

Jesus, being a man, taught us how to do it. The Lord's Prayer becomes our guide, our model prayer, found in Matthew 6:9-13.

There's no right or wrong formula when praying. We can't be sure as to whether our prayers will be answered or not. In fact, being in complete silence in the presence of God is a form of prayer, because He already knows what you need without having to open your mouth. When I'm feeling extremely down, I'd stay in peace and let His presence come to me without saying a word.

When prayer becomes your lifestyle, it feels more personal, as though you're talking to a friend where you can openly say anything—your victories, your failures, your disappointments, your hopes, and your dreams.

In prayer, adoration is a part where we venerate and worship God. Through adoration, we acknowledge God's worthiness to be exalted and glorified whether our prayers are answered or not. When we adore Him, we reflect upon His divine character—His holiness and goodness, mercy, power, grace, dominion, and love.

I've learned that, by devoting our prayer time every single day, thanking and adoring Him, a window is opened for abundant blessings to pour down. When we bless the Lord by speaking with our soul in it, it doesn't mean we make God strengthened or a better God, but rather it's our expression of praise about His greatness and goodness. Because the reality is, God is the primal and inexhaustible "source of blessings,"—meaning, He is already above everything in a blessed state, who is the fullness and the very main source of all our blessings.

An acquaintance provoked a debate and asked me once this question:

If God is already complete and self-sufficient, why does He still command us to praise and worship Him?

God's worthiness doesn't change whether we pray or not, worship Him or not. He doesn't need us, but we need Him! When we exalt Thy presence as our God, it blesses us; we get to enjoy and share His glory. In short, our praise is for our benefit and not God's.

Our Nothingness Without God

We have our worldly standards about excellence and failures. Our human nature longs for worldly praises through the accomplishments we've achieved thus far, leading to the dangers of arrogance, conceit, and pride—thinking that we are better than others. Jesus warns us against these things to regard ourselves as "somebody" and self-sufficient, which can destroy rather than build us.

However, when we mature in our Christian faith, we'd come to appreciate the transitory nature and value of strengthening our dependency on God, that we have our own sets of vulnerable attributes as part of our human existence and nature. We acquire the understanding that our time, talents, and treasure are God's gifts to us, and without Him, we are nothing.

I don't know if I should feel scared or proud, because innovations are nonstop. Although advanced technology is a byproduct of human intelligence, it disrupts some aspects of our wellbeing. Imagine this: artificial intelligence such as driverless cars can now replace a man's usual job. There will come a time where robots will be in the frontline to check your bank accounts.

At the time of this writing, global crisis is happening: fires, floods, volcanic eruptions, wars, diseases, and more. Can we control those?

No matter how high a man's intellectual potential is, he still doesn't have the capacity to calm the storm, or stop the volcanic eruption. Only God can do that.

"...so that at the name of Jesus every knee should bend, in heaven and on earth and under the earth, and every tongue should confess that Jesus Christ is Lord, to the glory of God the Father." – Philippians 2:10-11

I invite you to acknowledge our nothingness without God.

CONFESSION

To confess is to admit an offense, a transgression. In doing so, it provides a certain amount of relief and peace from the burden of carrying the guilt associated with it.

The Sacrament of Confession is one of the most unique aspects of Catholicism. Through the power of God vested upon the priest, we profess our faults for the forgiveness of sins.

Every time we exercise confession, we receive God's healing, grace, and mercy. It's our conscious initiative to reconcile with God, with the intention to sin no more. We are strengthened to resist temptations that confront us every single day.

Our Sinful Nature

We have our sinful nature injected into us through the original sin we inherited from Adam and Eve. When we sin, a barrier is created between us and God, interrupting our fellowship with Him. And that's exactly why we need to humble ourselves and admit our sinfulness through the act of contrition in the Sacrament of Penance, also known as confession.

Many ask—both Catholics and non-Catholics—why confessing sins needs to be done through a priest and not directly to God.

I asked a Catholic priest, and he said: "Yes, we've been given direct access to God through baptism in the Holy Spirit, and, through that, we are encouraged to use that access to apologize and repent of our sins. However, the role of the priests in our Christian faith answers the question as to why we need to go through them to confess. They stand as our symbolic mediator in the same way that the Word of God was written and not told to our generations directly, as our channel to know more about Him. God, during the Pentecost when He was risen from the dead, appeared before His apostles and gave them the ability to forgive sins, which then demonstrated that Jesus was instituting a new priesthood through them and extending His true and full forgiveness to those who come in repentance."

"If you forgive the sins of any, they are forgiven them; if you retain the sins of any, they are retained." – John 20:23

It made sense to me, and I hope it also did to you.

Let me ask you this:

When somebody has wronged or hurt you, you'd like that person to apologize or ask for forgiveness, right? Understandably, there are times when we can't freely give that forgiveness right away due to pain inflicted upon us. Whatever the case may be, God gave us that gift—the gift to forgive our brothers and sisters who have wronged us—which supports His Word written in John 20:23.

Confession is a must to reconcile with God and our fellowmen.

Unlimited Access

You are highly favored!

When we are forgiven, God forgets and erases our sins. We can absolutely start a new life with Jesus.

As Christians, our unlimited access to God's mercy and forgiveness doesn't justify that we are to sin as many times as we want.

Confession doesn't only bring us to forgiveness and absolution of sins but also to the state of God's grace. God frees us from the effects or consequences of sinning with His reminder to sin no more.

God really wants to bless us in all aspects, but sin blocks us from receiving those blessings. When we admit our sins and confess them, we are under His grace. And "grace" enables us to receive God's power and healing through the mercy of God.

When somebody pushes you in the long lineup at a store and you chose not to retaliate, that's grace. When you are cut off while driving and you chose to let it go, that's grace. In other words, spiritual or divine grace is a gift from God that enables us to resist temptations and exercise divine strength to pass the test. When we forgive others—regardless of whose fault it is— we become conduits of God's grace.

With repentance, God offers absolution of sins every single day—provided you access that.

THANKSGIVING

We celebrate Thanksgiving Day in Canada on the second Monday of October each year, which has become a tradition since the late 1950s.

It signifies a celebration for good harvest and prosperity in the past year.

We celebrate our birthdays not for the purpose of collecting gifts, but rather to commemorate our significant existence on this earth. It's also about giving thanks.

And talk about giving thanks—we express our feelings from being able to receive anything that makes us happy or delighted, expressed by the words, "Thank you!"

I believe that we can experience a more blessed life when we exercise this one thing after waking up each morning: The Attitude of Gratitude.

The Attitude of Gratitude

To possess an attitude of gratitude is to live your life from a place of being grateful for everything that is, regardless of your circumstances. It triggers your state of mind and your attitude towards a more holistic, healthy lifestyle than anything else available; it's a contagious, yet, a positive energy that humans can tap into.

When we say "thank you" to others as an expression of appreciation, not only do you feel good about it, but so does the person receiving your gratitude. It revitalizes our wellbeing.

As parents, we teach our children early on about the importance of saying the magic words such as "Please, Sorry, You're Welcome, and Thank You".

As Christians, giving thanks to God revitalizes our souls, because we acknowledge that His love endures forever, and that there's nothing we can or cannot do to change His love for us.

Our gratefulness makes us appreciate how much we do have instead of what we don't have. However, it doesn't mean that we should only give thanks to God under favorable conditions. We can still have grateful hearts even when we don't like our circumstances. We can get hurt but still feel thankful.

At the time of writing this part about thanking God in every circumstance, our doorbell rang. A lady stood by our door, holding a white envelope in her hand. I asked her to leave it in my mailbox. I took the mail and opened it. To my surprise, it was a letter from the Superior Court of Justice, concerning a real estate property for which I'm being sued.

I felt scared and was literally shaking.

And I thought to myself, "God, if this is a joke, it's not funny."

Imagine, I'm writing a book to start off my new year with a bang! But it turned out to be a different kind of a bang, so to speak.

I let things settle down and prayed, asking God for His wisdom.

Although I can't divulge the details of the said lawsuit, everything was dealt with appropriately by our legal counsel. And

I can't wait for the revised edition of this book to come out very soon such that I can reveal victory and God's glory, because I know God allowed this setback for a divine setup.

I learned about offering God a "sacrifice of praise," which means worshipping amidst tough times, as written in Hebrews 13:15 that says, "*Through him, then, let us continually offer a sacrifice of praise to God, that is, the fruit of lips that confess his name.*"

It is through difficult times that our attitude of gratitude is tested. God is not the author of our problems and challenges; however, He sometimes allows them to come into our lives to show Himself and what He can do for us. Of course, we don't thank God for these tribulations, but what we are thankful about is God's strength and endurance that He provides, so that we can climb our respective mountains, keeping our resentment at bay.

It made me realize that being grumpy when challenged requires the same energy with being thankful.

I know this is easier said than done, but trusting God makes a huge difference.

What's in It for Me

For the most part, it's our human nature that, when we give, we expect something in return, right? And it's where frustration comes to play.

I'm guilty of that. I have this WIIFM (What's in It for Me) attitude.

In business, I believe it's not bad at all. It just makes sense to know first what you'll get in exchange of either your time, money, or effort.

But giving thanks to God is different. Remember that you didn't ask for most of the things you have now in the first place; they were already given to you even before asking. And most importantly, when you give thanks to God, it doesn't cost you even a single penny.

So, what's in it for you to thank God in all circumstances?

When we thank Him, we bring Him closer into our lives. We make ourselves aware that His comforting presence is with us all the time.

We also view our challenges through a different perspective. We see the bigger picture, because we believe that these are just a part of God's master plan. He allows pains and troubles for His good purpose for us.

We easily become sidetracked when troubles come along our path, but thanking God enables us to focus on one subject only— God's Holy presence through gratefulness.

We are made humble through our total submission to God when we are grateful, recognizing God's will—and not ours—be done.

Gratefulness also creates that inner joy in our being, having that sense of deep reassurance that God is in control.

Giving thanks to God all the time also gives us an advantage over our foes. God never sleeps or slumbers, and He knows all our concerns. When everything on the surface seems unfavorable to us, God always has the final say. He's just and righteous. He knows His timing; not early or late, just right on time.

"If God is for us, who is against us?" – Romans 8:31

SUPPLICATION

We have different needs—for human beings to survive.

Abraham Maslow, an American psychologist, created the Maslow's hierarchy of needs that talks about a theory of psychological health predicted on fulfilling innate human needs in priority, culminating in self-actualization.

According to his theory, physiological needs are to be met first, as they are the very foundation of human survival that include food, water, clothes, and shelter.

Humans also have safety needs that include resources such as money, employment, security, and more.

Our social needs include love, sense of belonging, and intimacy.

We also require self-esteem needs, such as confidence, status, and respect.

Lastly, according to Maslow's theory, we have to achieve the self-actualization stage and live the best life towards fulfillment and creativity.

We definitely have different kinds of needs. Our daily lives operate on seeking answers for questions and needs to be met such that we can identify ourselves as happy at some level.

The Lord's Prayer

Found in the Gospel of Luke 11:1-4, Jesus taught us how to pray using The Lord's Prayer.

The prayer of supplication is an act of invocation to ask God to provide us with what we need.

And The Lord's Prayer is a strong demonstration of two things: who God is as our Father, and who we are as His Children that need prayer petitions.

Supplication is also known as petition, which literally means that one earnestly asks God to provide something for himself or for somebody else.

St. Thomas Aquinas, a Catholic priest, philosopher, and theologian, pointed out the order of our petitions to the Lord as perfectly laid out inside The Lord's Prayer, and they are as follows:

1) "Hallowed be Thy name," recognizing that God is Holy and we share with His Holiness.

2) "Thy kingdom come," by which we ask to come to the glory of His kingdom.

3) "Thy will be done on earth as it is in heaven."

4) "Give us this day our daily bread," asking for God's sustenance in both body and soul.

5) "Forgive us our trespasses as we forgive…," where we seek God's mercy to forgive and be forgiven.

6) "Lead us not into temptation," asking God to help us identify what leads us to sin and avoid them.

7) "Deliver us from evil," asking God to protect us and take us away from the spiritual battles caused by the evil ones.

Praying for Others

"*First of all, then, I urge that supplications, prayers, intercessions, and thanksgivings should be made for everyone, for kings and all who are in high positions, so that we may lead a quiet and peaceable life in all godliness and dignity.*" – 1 Timothy 1-2.

"Please pray for me."

Do you also say that? I do, most of the time.

Why do we still ask others to pray for us when, in fact, we can directly access God in prayer and do it ourselves, for ourselves, and by ourselves?

Life happens every single day. There are times when we feel as though we're trapped in a pile of troubles, in that we can't seem to breathe at all; we're all choked up—leaving us desperate and hopeless. Thus, we seek relief, a moment of ease.

More often than not, we turn to something that gives us comfort. And asking for a prayer from others close to us gives us that.

We don't just pray for others who are still alive; we also do pray for those who have departed this earth.

So, why pray for others?

First, we need to pray for others because Jesus Christ commanded us to do so—enemies included. When we pray for others, we also participate with God in the ministry of reconciliation as a means to bring others to repentance and salvation in Jesus Christ. We also become prayer warriors for others, so that we can actively participate in God's plan for the world, including our lives and the lives of others. Praying for others is also an act of love, because it shifts our focus off of ourselves and gives way onto the needs of others around us instead. By praying for others, we help to build up the body of Christ.

REFLECTION

What does reflection mean?

According to Merriam-Webster Dictionary, it is a thought, idea, or opinion formed or a remark made as a result of meditation.

In the spiritual realm, it means a serious consideration or a thought about something. It involves deep contemplation and meditation in prayer.

Religious debates and divisions in Christianity arise, because of different interpretations of the scripture. Some take the passages at their literal meaning, while some take them out of context. So, it's not a surprise that we now have thousands of Christian denominations all over the world.

I'll tell you again that I'm not a Bible expert or a theologian. And that's the reason why I was initially hesitant to write this book. There's a huge responsibility associated with doing it. I know there's God, but I'm afraid to have misunderstood His Word.

I reflected upon His message on how to get this book done. And now I get it.

He wants me to share my story and how He worked and continues to work in me.

Yes, I've written down some biblical passages here. I have my Holy Bible with me as I write to check on them for accuracy's sake. When I'd write about an event or an experience in my life under a specific topic, a clear message will just be downloaded to me, as though somebody is telling me to look it up in the Holy Bible to support it.

Isn't that amazing?

I called one of my spiritual advisors and asked for guidance, as I felt I have run out of strength to continue, with feelings of heightened anxiety, worries, and stress. I was told that God wants this book to be more meaningful in such a way that He can communicate clearly His divine message to you and me. I was advised to go on, assuring me that God will vindicate me and restore me for His purpose.

In fact, this book was written in roughly two weeks amidst my unstable emotional and mental states. I felt so much inspiration despite being sued while chasing after a staff who ran away with our money of several months' worth of rent from one of our rental properties, because my BIG BOSS got me covered.

My most favorite biblical verse is Romans 8:28:

"And we know that all things work together for good for those who Love God, who are called according to his purpose."

Our harmonious relationship with God requires us to act on deepening our spiritual growth with Him by reflecting on His Word.

And here are some of the ways we can do that:

For my daily Bible reading guide, I use *Didache*, which is a devotional booklet with biblical passages for the whole year and reflections of ordinary people with their ordinary circumstances.

We also can benefit from attending the Holy Mass where priests in the Liturgy of the Holy Word give us reflections, interpretations, and instructions about the particular reading for the day.

We also have the opportunity to learn from a gathering to study the Bible in our respective communities or groups.

The Holy Spirit provides us inspirations to reflect on God's Word all the time.

Being reflective is also being receptive to God's message through our surroundings.

Daily reflection about our lives is also needed. A thorough self-audit, including our activities, thoughts, feelings, encounters with self and others, and motives before going to sleep at night can help redirect us towards becoming better individuals the next day.

A Life of Prayer

Can you still remember when you first fell in love with another person? You probably wished that the feeling of ecstasy would stay forever. You've always wanted to be connected to that person, as though you're the only ones in the world. You just hoped that the clock would stop. Isn't it?

Falling in love with God is the same thing. We develop a life of prayer because it's our means to communicate directly with Him. It's our devoted time to talk to Him exclusively.

As Christians, we'll grow our intimate relationship with God as we take the time to talk to Him each day through a life of prayer. In doing so, we'll learn how to become more intentional in listening and responding to His leading. We become open and sensitive to His messages through prompts or signs—both tangible and intangible.

A life of prayer also strengthens our faith as our stronghold through which God speaks to us and continuously reveals Himself within the depths of our conscience. Because when He does this, we manifest faith by responding to all that He reveals to us.

CHAPTER 3

IMITATE

WE KNOW THAT ALL CHILDREN GO THROUGH THEIR RESPECTIVE growth and developmental milestones at different ages and stages. These stages include physical, cognitive, emotional, social, language, sensory, and motor development.

Although learning skills may differ from one child to another, generally speaking, all can naturally and easily adapt to the environment that they're in—their household, for instance. The critical stage runs between ages two and five, where they start to explore and imitate almost everything they see, regardless if it's safe or not, good or bad.

As a parent, it's important that I become consciously aware of what I think, say, and how I act because my children copy and imitate me for the most part, whether I like it or not.

The perceptions that they've collected from their developmental stage will significantly affect their upbringing and outlook in life.

Imitating can be a bad thing at times; for instance, when it comes to counterfeiting items like bags, shoes, beauty products.

Not only do these fake or pirated commodities destroy their original brands, but also the ones patronizing them. When quality is compromised, the negative effects can go as far as destroying health, relationships, and reputations.

On the other hand, I watch and observe successful people. Although I know that success is a process and takes time, I've learned that there's a smarter and faster way to achieve one's goals and dreams. How? By copying or imitating the successful people's strategies in your niche or area of interest. When I say imitating, it doesn't mean stealing their copyrighted content, their signature products, or their identity, but rather making them as your role model and applying their principles towards reaching your level of success in your own right.

BEING ONE OF US

Fulfilling a sense of belonging is a human need. It's within our nature to want to be accepted. We long to fit in and be part of a certain network or group. And when we do, we tend to upgrade ourselves so much that we are caught up with the higher expectations of the patriarchs or matriarchs in the family, bosses at work, and community leaders.

We see and read horrible stories of such in movies, soap operas, and books.

Part of our Christian faith is to believe the unthinkable— something like our God who sits in the highest throne and the creator of the universe and everything in it—visible and nonvisible—would be born in a lowly stable some two thousand years ago.

But why?

"For in Him the whole fullness of deity dwells bodily…" – Colossians 2:9

Jesus Christ became physically human while He's also fully divine through the process of incarnation; in other words, Jesus is God in the flesh.

It's been a joke around but partly true that when you criticize yourself, you're actually criticizing the One who made you. From that perspective, every human being is God's masterpiece that nobody should ever devaluate, because the potter is great!

Because of God's love for us, He downgraded Himself to our level for the reasons that He wanted to further reveal God to us in a manner that we can comprehend and understand. He also came to our being to fulfill His promise of bringing salvation to all humanity by dying on the cross, which also fulfills a new covenant with us. The aim of His coming was also to destroy the works of the devil. Jesus stood as our role model that we can imitate through His examples of good deeds and His humility while being a human in flesh and blood. Jesus came to earth to prepare humanity for their heavenly destiny, which is Holiness.

Your True Purpose

Let me go back to this biblical passage I mentioned previously:

"Then God said, "Let us make humankind in our image, according to our likeness; and let them have dominion over the fish of the sea, and over the birds of the air, and over the cattle, and over all wild animals of the earth, and over every creeping thing that creeps upon the earth. So, God created humankind in His image, in the image of God he created them; male and female he created them." – Genesis 1:26-27

You see, we, humans, are created in God's own image and likeness for our true purpose. And being the highest form of all His creations, we have the ability to think, speak, and feel. Because of that, we're given the authority to rule and reign over other creatures. We are God's representatives to exhibit stewardship over all His creations.

He did not just randomly choose you and me for nothing, because He has a purpose for our existence. Jesus Christ revealed that purpose to His disciples at their last meal together.

"My Father is glorified by this, that you bear much fruit and become my disciples." – John 15:8

And the essence of God's plan and purpose for humankind is for us to bear much fruit, created in Jesus Christ for good works. The Lord wants us to live a godly and a spiritually productive life.

As His children, He wants us to have a fruitful living, not the kind of living that the world described it to be. When we follow the world's standards of being fruitful, it brings nothing but only discontentment. However, when we allow God to live in us through the guidance of the Holy Spirit, bearing much fruit can truly be manifested because only the Holy Spirit can produce the real fruit.

"By contrast, the fruit of the Spirit is love, joy, peace, patience, kindness, generosity, faithfulness, gentleness, and self-control." – Galatians 5:22

We know that God is divine and holy, righteous and good. Ideas and concepts like justice, truth, and morality relate to God—and we, humans, have the capacity to identify such concepts.

"Humans are not only created by God but also for God, which states: "…for in Him all things in heaven and on earth were created, things visible and invisible, whether thrones or dominions or rulers or powers – all things have been created through Him and for Him." – Colossians 1:16

Because of that, the true and high purpose is ascribed only to humankind as eternal beings; it is not present in animals or other living creatures on earth.

As we share in His image and likeness, we are called to imitate God's divine nature towards eternity.

God is glorified when we bear much fruit and become His disciples.

THE WORKS OF MERCY

"Servants are not greater than their Master. If they persecuted me, they will persecute you; if they kept my word, they will keep yours also." – John 15:20

God is our creator and the master of the universe and everything in it. As part of our calling to fulfill our true purpose, we are also called to imitate His good deeds through the works of mercy.

The works of mercy are meritorious acts of both penance and charity towards our brethren, which Jesus Christ demonstrated when He did His ministry work on earth.

How can we share good deeds to others?

Humans have body, mind, and spirit—thus, there are needs to be met, which we can fulfill through the examples of Jesus.

Corporal and Spiritual

As I've mentioned previously, our different types of needs

include the physical. This type of need is what the corporal works of mercy do to help our brothers and sisters satisfy the needs of their physical bodies.

The Corporal Works of Mercy are specifically written in the Gospel of Matthew 25:35-36, "...*for I was hungry and you gave me food, I was thirsty and you have me something to drink, I was a stranger and you welcomed me, I was naked and you gave me clothing, I was sick and you took care of me, I was in prison and you visited me...*"

We are called to imitate God's examples and share our blessings with others, especially with those who are in desperate need. We may have our own issues, challenges, and shortages of supplies, but God—in His simplicity and modesty as a human being without any taste of luxury as a man—still managed to demonstrate good deeds for others.

In doing the same, we also share with God's mercy that's made available to us through our display of selfless loving by giving and sharing.

Aside from the works of mercy that help the physical matter, we can also help our brothers and sisters in Christ with their emotional and spiritual needs that are collectively known as "the Spiritual Works of Mercy".

When we instruct the ignorant, we share about the Gospel and how to live it by our mere examples. We're also called to counsel the doubtful when they are troubled and confused. Forgiveness, as human beings, is one of the hardest things to do; however, God's mercy affords us the strength to fulfill this spiritual act.

According to a proverbial phrase, "To err is human; to forgive is divine." To admonish the sinner is simply helping somebody who has fallen off track to get back on the path towards holiness. We are also called to bear wrongs patiently when we face injustice. Praying for both the living and the dead is also an act of spiritual mercy.

All the works of mercy—both corporal and spiritual—are our means to draw closer to God to know Him and be like Him.

DYING TO ONESELF

"Then he said to them all, 'If any want to become my followers, let them deny themselves and take up their cross daily and follow me.'" – Luke 9:23

What the world now teaches us is that we become attached to material things, instead of the things that really matter, mostly for personal gain. However, God's Word says otherwise—to die to oneself. This requires obedience, and it's not easy.

Our carnal mind is so corrupted by greed, ego, pride, and selfishness that block us from obeying God's will. It's the very nature of every human being to "do things his way."

A baby cries for different reasons—signaling hunger, painful stimuli in the body, discomfort, or anything—to grab the mother's attention. The baby wants attention, full attention. If you're also a mother, you know exactly what I mean. Babies want to be the center of your world; they are oblivious to everything else.

We are called by God to do the opposite. He knows every concern we have in our lives. And it would be far from the truth to not be distracted by looking for resolutions for our own challenges before we can focus our attention to others.

It even becomes more challenging when He said to not only deny ourselves but to take up the cross and follow Him—mind you, not just once, but daily. That sounds pretty heavy to me.

Less is More

"Travel light." Fr. Jerry Orbos, SVD, shared this message in one of his inspirational talks as we approached the new year.

My family and I love to travel, but packing for a family of six is stressful. And I learned to have a list of what to bring handy as a reminder, so that I wouldn't forget items. However, I learned another strategy that is less stressful and less expensive: travel light —to only bring the very basics of everything.

Distractions. We experience them all the time. And distractions mostly come from the past. We cling to them too much, which hinder us from moving on. And in doing so, we are missing out on what's waiting for us in the now. Fr. Jerry Orbos advises us to be here and to be present now, because God is here. Yesterday is a past event, including your mistakes, failures, and pains. There's a new story to unfold in your life today.

When I also started to focus on my life's priorities and what matters to me more, I embraced the concept of minimalism. I began to practice it by decluttering my own closet, to our household items and everything else around the house. I've come to appreciate the beauty in simple living—less distractions. Open physical space invites clarity, especially in decision-making.

When things don't turn out the way we expect them to go, we hold grudges against ourselves, others, and sometimes God.

When Jesus instructed us to follow Him and take up our cross every day, He simply meant that we must be willing to get past the pains of being judged, persecuted, and treated unjustly. We're invited to give way and to die to ourselves, and be denied of comfort, honor, sometimes human approval, and life.

We play victims of the circumstances. And that robs us of peace and harmony to live one day at a time. Remember, what we have is just today, because yesterday is already gone and tomorrow is yet to come—or, who knows; it may never come.

We are called to trust the cross and follow Him, instead of giving in to our own desires.

We are invited to live simply, so that we can focus on loving more—not just ourselves but others as well.

Travel light, because less is more.

A MAN OF HIS WORD

There's nothing as painful as having been lied to or cheated on, especially when the hurt was caused by our most trusted people.

As parents, we can't seem to always keep our promises to our children—not because we'd like to play games with them, but circumstances do happen. But they remember those broken promises, whether or not they understand the reasons behind our failure to keep our word.

Almost every one of us is guilty of not keeping our promises, which negatively affects our credibility to other people.

But I know of One—just One—who never breaks His promises. He is a man of His Word, and His name is Jesus.

God's Faithfulness

"God is faithful; by him you were called into the fellowship of his Son, Jesus Christ our Lord." – 1 Corinthians 1:9

God promised that anyone who seeks Him, can find Him. There are literally many biblical passages about His faithfulness.

Faith is a gift to begin with; and as we grow in faith, we become more familiar with God's promises.

But why does it really matter to us if God is being always faithful to His promises?

The answer is simple: His faithfulness speaks about His divine character. He's the same God yesterday, today, and forever. He hasn't changed even a bit, which means that His Word remains the same until the end of time.

What does God's faithfulness do to us?

There are far too many reasons, but I'd highlight some.

God's faithfulness is never dependent upon whether we're faithful or not. In fact, our human nature has too many flaws, and our faithfulness is far from perfect. His faithfulness will never match ours.

His faithfulness protects us from temptations. When we hold on to God's promise, we can access His mighty power to reject thoughts and acts of sin.

God is the God of abundance, and His faithfulness never runs out. His supply is unlimited.

When we trust God's faithfulness, we develop our personal relationship and fellowship with Him.

God's perfect faithfulness gives us hope. You'll become more aware of His promises and how His faithfulness is active in you when you mirror your life to His Word in the scripture.

CHAPTER 4

RESURRECT

What comes to your mind first when you hear the word "resurrect"?

I'd say, "to bring back to life".

It's our belief as Christians that Jesus Christ was raised from the dead three days after He was crucified.

In fact, we celebrate this most significant event in whole of the Christian Church as a festival and holiday, called Easter or Resurrection Sunday.

To resurrect is also synonymous with a state of restoration.

So, how can being resurrected or restored exhibit a life in sync with God?

BEING BORN AGAIN

"Jesus answered him, 'Very truly, I tell you, no one can see the kingdom of God without being born from above." – John 3:3

Jesus Christ, during His ministry work, would employ a creative method to articulate His message to people through stories inside the parables.

A parable is an ordinary earthly story that relates a heavenly value or meaning.

According to Matthew 13:10, Jesus's disciples even asked Him why He'd speak to them in parables. And Jesus answered them about the purpose of the parables, as follows:

"The reason I speak to them in parables is that seeing they do not perceive, and hearing they do not listen, nor do they understand." – Matthew 13:13

Jesus didn't intend to hide the truth about God's kingdom—it's just that the people are unwilling to receive His message, and that led them to misunderstand what He really meant to say.

It reminds me of one parable in the Holy Bible when Nicodemus, a Pharisee, visited Jesus one night.

"'Very truly, I tell you, no one can see the kingdom of God without being born from above.' Nicodemus said to him, 'How can anyone be born after having grown old? Can one enter a second time into the mother's womb and be born? Jesus answered, 'Very truly, I tell you, no one can enter the kingdom of God without being born of water and Spirit.'" – John 3:4-6

When we become inactive and complacent with our faith and do nothing about it, we die spiritually. And we're invited by God to renew our fellowship with Him by baptism in the Holy Spirit— thus being born again.

Water represents God's Word as the living water that quenches our thirst for the truth. Because true rebirth means gaining a new life with Jesus. Our world has corrupted humankind with evil disposition, such as greed, jealousy, deceit, and arrogance. We know that sin takes us away from God's kingdom. And for us to return, Jesus Christ demanded that we must be born again within God's Word and the Holy Spirit to have the divine life and not the worldly kind of life.

Your Breakthroughs

I love listening to Bishop Robert Barron's speeches for my spiritual alignment. He has a very insightful reflection about what it really meant to be born again in relation to Nicodemus's encounter with Jesus one night.

Bishop Barron highlighted some important areas in the whole passage. The word "night" signifies darkness—spiritual darkness— coming to Jesus, being the light.

It's our human nature to look for something that creates excitement and curiosity that triggers us to explore more. When boredom kicks in, we break a routine for a different outcome.

Either intentional or not, we discover something—also called our breakthroughs or aha moments.

I love attending live events, trainings, and workshops for my personal development. Although they may seem time-consuming and expensive for some, I find them useful to help me with my motivation and discovering my breakthroughs.

Our goal to gain wealth, pleasure, honor, and power is the worldly breakthrough—Bishop Robert Barron said that these are not bad things. He reiterated that our human nature remains, but the good thing about it is that, while we work on those worldly breakthroughs, our perspective about them change when we let God's grace fill our lives with guidance through our spiritual breakthrough. In doing so, we aim to do more, because we want to give more and bless others more. We are then restored to a new creation, as we feel everything in a different way. We understand our lives differently. Because we experience a transformation of consciousness below the surface, the Holy Spirit enables to transfigure our old self, thus making us a new creation—a transformed one, a restored spirit.

We are invited to cooperate with the Holy Spirit, so that our spiritual breakthrough is manifested into our life.

In our pursuit of earthly breakthroughs, we seek wisdom from more successful people to teach us and guide us as to how they'd arrived to that path.

The same works with our spiritual breakthrough, which can only happen by seeking God's wisdom. When we have our spiritual highs, we become receptive to God's messages that subsequently develop our personal relationship with Him.

A GLIMMER OF HOPE

"For there is hope for a tree, if it is cut down, that it will sprout again." – Job 14:7

Our world is chaotic, corrupted, and divided. It seems as though only a few are favored and the rest is left with nothing to choose from.

Hopelessness is a dreaded feeling of despair and feeling stuck. It feels like we have nothing to live for, and that becomes both all-consuming and life-threatening.

Nobody is spared from this, and it just comes to us in different times and seasons. I have my own season—who doesn't?

When I was still suffering from Postpartum Depression, I felt gloomy and hopeless. It was not just a feeling of desperation, but also of fear. I was consumed by uncertainties about everything—fear of the unknown. Until I held on to that one weapon: my faith in God. It gave me the courage to rise above the depression, knowing that God will fight not just for me but with me.

I cut myself out of the agony by giving myself the permission to rise—just like a tree that requires some trimming to remove unproductive branches, but I didn't do it alone. I sought God's help through a wonderful gift of faith—faith that breeds courage to be resilient and rise above my challenges.

Confident Expectations

When I reached my early thirties, I had experienced sudden acne breakouts, which I never had when I was younger. I sought different medical experts' advice to solve the problem, but to no avail. I tried many topical creams and pills but landed on the same fate. Until one day, I chanced upon an online advertisement, talking about my problem—acne. I became so enthused by it and finished the forty-five-minute presentation. My excitement heightened even more because the product was endorsed by a successful celebrity, and I thought to myself, "This is it!" In short, I was sold and bought the products at once.

You see, I've had my confident expectations, not because of the product itself but because of the endorser. And, I believe, this strategy works very well in business. We buy because we trust.

We have the same confident expectations about God's goodness and what He can do in our lives. But the problem with humankind is, we pin our hopes on material things and to people—both of which have expiry dates. It's our very nature, as we want to do things our way. We lack patience. We want things done now! We fail to realize that God's timing is perfect—never early or never too late. He's just right on time!

Our earthly definition of hope is limited, as we are not sure as to whether it's coming true or not.

"I hope to pass the test." "I hope to be rich in five years." "I hope that my boss approves my vacation."

These are common lines in our everyday living, as we associate our hopes with uncertainties—meaning, we can't put our 100% faith in them. It coincides with the line, "Hoping for the best." Because in reality, nobody hopes for the worst.

But God's definition of hope is different. Being a God of absolutes, He will never ever change His plan and purpose for all of us. And if we put our confidence to expect things to happen for us based on those two immutable promises, we can never be swayed by any force in the world. We'll possess the indwelling strength from God.

When we put our hope in God, we don't cross our fingers because we are certain that everything is transferred to His very capable hands of doing great things for us, as He promised in Jeremiah 29:11, *"For surely I know the plans I have for you, says the Lord, plans for your welfare and not for harm, to give you a future with hope."*

LIFE AFTER DEATH

Mortality. Everything that has a life has to die or come to an end.

When I was in the pre-Medicine school in university back in the day, we learned about human body cells, their morphology, and their life cycle.

A red blood cell, for instance, is made in the stem cells of the bone marrow. The immature red blood cell undergoes a process called erythropoiesis to become a mature red blood cell that produces hemoglobin. Hemoglobin carries oxygen throughout the body. A mature red blood cell has a life span of about 120 days before it is removed from the circulation through different body organs like the spleen, liver, and bone marrow. This expired cell is then broken down to produce other components (heme and globin from hemoglobin), which produce essential elements like bilirubin and iron plus amino acids. Most of these elements are recycled and will enter the circulation again—for instance, in the bone marrow—to be used in the production of a new red blood cell again.

In the same way that plants bear fruits with seeds that are then sown to germinate a new plant, their life cycle goes on.

I know this is quite technical, medically speaking, but my point is this: there's something coming out after a certain life expires. God designed it that way.

We'll all die; that's very certain. And only God knows when and how.

We knew stories in the Holy Bible where dead people were raised back to life by Jesus. And we also know now that when a person is dead, that's it—at least, in the physical world.

"And just as it is appointed for mortals to die once, and after that judgment…" – Hebrews 9:27

Eternal Life

"For the wages of sin is death, but the free gift of God is eternal life in Christ Jesus our Lord." – Romans 6:23

I paid my last respect to one of my friends' father who died of cancer many, many years ago. I was prepared to see the usual ambiance of such event with sad faces, people crying and mourning. A few steps away, I could already hear the noise and music coming from the viewing room. It was the exact opposite of what I had initially expected. The eulogy was commenced by a very touching speech that talked about celebration of life after death. The speaker went on to say that death is not the end of the journey, but rather the beginning of something better—eternal life.

It was a very moving speech that changed my perspective about death.

Eternal life is God's promise, but not everyone can taste that promise. Because of man's refusal to reconcile with God, we'll surely miss out on our divine opportunity to share His glory in God's kingdom.

When we acknowledge and confess our sins to reunite with God, He will forgive us instantly and wash us of all our old ways and wickedness. We can also enjoy being adopted into the family of God. In the Christian sense, eternal life has a deathless duration, which relates to God's kind of eternity.

It was a very touching story when Jesus was crucified alongside two thieves and one of them acknowledged his sins, asked for God's forgiveness, and sought God's kingdom. Jesus, despite His suffering on the cross, gave a beautiful picture of God's love and mercy.

"Then he said, 'Jesus, remember me when you come into your kingdom.' He replied, 'Truly I tell you, today you will be with me in Paradise.'" – Luke 23:42

God showed His unconditional love and mercy for us, no matter how grave our sins are, so long that we are penitent and sorry for our sins.

We are also invited to do the same.

I AM FREE

"Free is good."

"The best things in life are free."

I hear these lines all the time.

Due to huge competition in the market these days, entrepreneurs stretch their marketing strategies to win customers, which are largely applicable to online marketing. The reality is, rapport needs to be established first before your prospective clients will trust you. And the most effective way to do that is by providing them with "FREE" stuff like an e-book, cheat sheet, worksheets, webinars, or trainings. Remember the "What's in It for Me" strategy?

But, hey, is there really such a thing as FREE?

I delivered a speech some months ago about this argument as to whether or not free stuff really exist.

I have to remind you, though, that this is just my personal opinion and I'm not saying I'm absolutely right.

"*There's nothing free in this world,*" I said as the opening words of my speech.

Your free e-book, that's not really free. Your free headphone with your cell phone is also not free. Your free socks with your shirt, not free either.

Here's why:

When you signed up for that free e-book, you gave your e-mail and name, right? The person who created that "free e-book" exhausted his resources such as time, effort, and money, right?

Your free headphone required other resources to have it manufactured, isn't it?

The company that included that free stuff to your cell phone must have purchased that item, probably at a wholesale price.

Am I making sense here?

In other words, a trade must have happened before it's delivered to you and perceived as FREE.

Many people are jealous of our healthcare system here in Canada. We don't really pay for most of our medical expenses and other medications, but are they free? Nah. Not a chance.

I worked in the corporate world for many, many years. I paid huge taxes, and part of that goes to our healthcare budget.

What about this one:

They said that air is free. But who created the air? Of course, God.

It just means that it may not be too obvious to see who spent for this and that, but one thing is for sure: somebody must have paid the price in advance.

We are freed from our sinfulness. Who paid for it at the highest cost?

Freedom Spelled

Whenever I see the cross, I see freedom. Why?

Other Christians and non-believers criticize Catholics because of their strong display and demonstration of the physical cross in churches and religious items, in addition to doing the sign of the cross when praying—in the Name of the Father, and of The Son, and of The Holy Spirit.

This is the practice I was born to, and I'll be bold to honestly say that I have no intention to change it regardless.

Bishop Robert Barron explained that the physical cross that Catholics use is necessary to remind us of God's love despite every dysfunction of human beings thrown at Jesus through His death on the cross.

You must have seen the movie, *The Passion of the Christ*, where Jim Caviezel played the role of Jesus. It was directed by Mel Gibson, an American actor and filmmaker. It was really heartbreaking.

But because of that cross, I am free, and so are you. There's salvation in the cross—you and I are saved.

Somebody was crucified and died to set you and me free. It's the compelling truth that He gave His life for the forgiveness of our sins, because when we are forgiven, we are FREE.

If I'd spell freedom, I'd do it this way: C – R – O – S – S.

C – Christ
R – Redeemed
O – Our
S – Souls &
S – Set us FREE.

THE TRUTH

The truth will set you free.

"Then Jesus said to the Jews who had believed in him, 'If you continue in my word, you are truly my disciples; and you will know the

truth, and the truth will set you free." – John 8:31-32

But what's the truth? You may ask.

Seeking the truth is a basic human preoccupation. We do that in our lives every single day.

It's my practice to check my children's bags and lunch boxes after school.

One afternoon, as I was busy with other household tasks, I forgot to inspect my youngest child's bag. The next morning came and it was time for me to put in their new sets of lunches, when suddenly my son began to cry. Clueless what it was about, I asked him what happened or if he was hurting somewhere. He grabbed his bag while crying and showed me the smelly, rotten food still in the lunch box, untouched. Our house rule is to never lie, and my children know that we have a way to find out if they do. So, they're warned to tell the truth at once or they suffer the consequences.

We always seek the truth in our daily living—be it in relationships, parenting, work, school, business, etc.

Finding the truth seems to be harder these ways, as there are so many ways to conceal it—connections, money, popularity.

Trials in courts go haywire to defend cases where the true criminals are freed while innocent people are convicted. Because of that, justice is not properly served; and the sad reality is, laws are bent in favor of a few.

This may be the sad truth in the physical world, but, as Christians, there's one factual truth that cannot be concealed: God is alive who redeemed us from our sins.

"For the wages of sin is death, but the free gift of God is eternal life in Christ Jesus our Lord." – Romans 6:23

And that's what Jesus accomplished on the cross.

Living out The Truth Today

In today's very challenging world, it would be next to impossible to maintain proper composure all the time, which made me think that maybe being in the position of God is really, really hard.

But there you have it. Because the truth is, God is God and we can never be Him or replace His divine place.

To live out the truth now goes back to our God-given purpose and why we exist.

Let me take you back to John 15:8, which says, *"My Father is glorified by this, that you bear much fruit and become my disciples."*

Just like a plant, it won't grow and bear fruit without supplying its needs to survive—water, sun, air, and other nutrients to live.

We can't bear fruit on our own, because the fruit comes from the Holy Spirit—love, joy, peace, patience, kindness, goodness, faithfulness, gentleness, and self-control.

My husband's father left them for another woman back in the day. My husband was just a little boy when it happened. It hurt him deeply and hated him for a long time. When his father was diagnosed with cancer months before dying, my husband was able to forgive and reconcile with him on his deathbed.

That's how we can live out the truth today. We can't do incredible things on our own. We all need God's grace and mercy to do divine things such as forgiveness.

God said that we can never defeat the enemy's works by its own weapons.

"You have heard that it was said, 'An eye for an eye and a tooth for a tooth. But I say to you, do not resist an evildoer. But if anyone strikes you on the right cheek, turn the other also; and if anyone wants to sue you and take your coat, give your coat as well; and if anyone forces you to go one mile, go also the second mile." – Matthew 38-41

Spiritual Warfare

I'm not a fan of watching sports, involving close-body contacts, such as wrestling and boxing. They seem quite brutal to me—sorry, it's just me. It just freaks me out to see blood oozing from different parts of the body.

It's the physical world kind of battle—sports or real life.

However, there's another battle between good and evil in the spiritual realm, which we, humans, are fighting every single day. And that's our huge problem!

Why is it a problem?

Because the devil is a big deceiver whose main goal is to keep us away from the love of God through his lies. And when we're away from God, we're prisoners of sin.

Spiritual warfare is going on in the unseen world that is usually manifested in our damaged relationships, mental instability, emotional challenges, and physical exhaustion, as well as financial constraints and other areas of life. When one is stricken by the spirit outside of the Holy Spirit, he feels pinned down by resentment, anger, pride, deceit, insecurity, greed, unforgiveness, fear, and the list goes on.

"…for the weapons of our warfare are not merely human, but they have divine power to destroy strongholds." – 2 Corinthians 10:4

So, what's the solution to this?

Know the truth. The truth lies in what Jesus Christ's death accomplished on the cross to defeat all evil in the world. And through that, we are made victorious.

"…nor height, nor depth, nor anything else in all creation, will be able to separate us from the love of God in Christ Jesus our Lord." – Romans 8:39

CHAPTER 5

INTERCEDE

W HAT DOES INTERCEDE MEAN?

According to Merriam-Webster Dictionary, it means to intervene between parties with a view to reconciling differences. It also means to mediate.

One of the hardest moments of being a mother to my four young children is when all of them fight altogether. This is the time when I'd literally just like to walk away and forget about the world—just for a second. However, I am their mom, their mediator. I'm also their judge and it's my job to hear every side of the story.

I don't really play favoritism, because they're all my children. Favoritism hurts feelings, and I don't want that. So, being there to intercede while being fair is a very serious task.

How can the act of interceding or mediating be an image of a life in sync with God?

MY BROTHER'S KEEPER

"Then the Lord said to Cain, 'Where is your brother Abel?' He said, 'I do not know; am I my brother's keeper?'" – Genesis 3:9

We know the story in the scripture about Cain murdering his brother, Abel. And God—being God who knows everything—asked the question where his brother was. It was, in fact, an opportunity for Cain to confess the crime, but he refused to do so.

In our modern language today, it's an expression to excuse ourselves from our care with our brothers and sisters in Christ. Although under normal circumstances, we aren't the literal keepers of our neighbors; we are called as Christians to be mindful about the needs of others and to love them as ourselves, and taking their best interests at heart.

Your First Church

When I was younger, I thought that church literally meant a physical establishment or building where a religious worship is done. And I suppose, if you were to ask other people as well, you'd get varying responses.

The word "church" in the Holy Bible comes from the Greek word "ecclesia," which means a congregation or an assembly of citizens of an ancient Greek state. In other words, it simply refers to "people".

There are far more layers to the biblical view of the church, but I'd just highlight what church is to me as a mother and a wife in my household—my first church.

My calling is to become a wife and a mom; these are the significant roles I play every single day.

I decided to leave my corporate job to serve God through my family. I believe it's my moral obligation to maintain a haven of love inside my household because God lives in our church.

I'm not here to judge. I don't know about you, but this is what I believe. We can't say that we're truly serving God when our relationship with our family members is broken, or at least not given a chance to get it fixed. But sometimes, when issues arise that seem to be irreconcilable, we can still choose to forgive. It's not our job to change people, it's God's. Our job is to love them in spite of their flaws, even if it's from a distance.

I strive to operate based on this important fact: "You can't give what you don't have."

"...leave your gift there before the altar and go; first be reconciled to your brother or sister, and then come and offer your gift." – Matthew 5:24

An activity like going to our place of worship is highly encouraged for our spiritual growth with God and our brothers and sisters in Christ. However, most of the time, we tend to forget our first ministry inside our first church.

I hear stories of people who'd be in churches almost every single day while leaving unresolved issues at home.

As Mother Theresa said, "*If you want to change the world, go home and love your family.*"

There's no such thing as a perfect family; we know that. We fight; we argue. But that doesn't mean we can't love. And the family is the basic unit of our society. Being a mom and my husband's partner to raise our young family is a form of worship. After I deal with whatever I need to resolve inside my first church, then I'd be more capable of serving others outside my fence.

My family is my first ministry; here I have the opportunity to teach my children moral values and everything about God.

Jesus is the Light of the world, and I, with my husband, stand as the light to our household where we can lead our flock to our main Shepherd.

I sin and fall many times in a given day, but it doesn't prevent me from interceding for God through the first ministry that He gave me to love and to serve.

My church is not the institution; it's the people of God, whom I call my family—related in blood or not—who are united in the Holy Spirit.

God's Call to Warriors

We are called to be God's witnesses of His goodness and Good News—as warriors —and that's our purpose.

As Christians, we've been anointed to be soldiers in the army of God to fight against evil and its wrongdoings to defend His kingdom. And being a warrior comes with a huge responsibility. But the good news is, we don't have to do it alone. God equips us with everything we need to be prepared in the battlefield. We have a Great Commander who tasted death for every man; He stands as the captain of our salvation. Our identity stands out in the army as children of God. Being prepared to fight the spiritual warfare requires endurance by the power of the Holy Spirit as our guide. Lastly, our full protection is provided when we don the armor of God, holding the girdle of truth that the Living God is the one we serve and that our salvation depends on Him alone.

In our everyday lives, we fail all the time—one after the other. It's tedious, endless, frustrating, and exhausting. On the other hand, there are moments when, while fighting our own battles, we are also called to help others resolve their own.

Now, what?

The difference lies in remaining God-centered amidst life's chaos, focusing on the light of Jesus.

That's the quality of being God's warriors, and we are all called to be exactly that—to be in a position where God can fight all our battles for us.

HE MEETS WHERE YOU ARE

I could still remember when Chris, my husband, was still courting me many, many years ago. It would take him hours just to get to my house to visit and see me. It was one of the sweetest things, and I loved him for it to this day.

As a human being, when you love someone, you'd do everything with all your power and might to express your feelings whether it's reciprocated or not. Love is selfless. It reflects you and what you can do for the one you love.

God is the same, although His kind of love can never be compared to the kind of love we have as human beings. He knows our limitations, our shortcomings, our sinfulness, our failures. But despite that, He's into you. He's madly in love with you. And because He loves you, He meets where you are. He embraces all the flaws —every single thing.

Your Flaws for His Glory

A renewed life in the Holy Spirit is waiting for us.

We cannot hide from the Lord. He knows us from head to toe, every strand of our hair—our strengths, our weaknesses, our flaws.

But do you know that God also uses our flaws for His glory to bless others, too?

You may have heard of different stories in the Holy Bible about Jesus's disciples whom He hand-picked and associated Himself with. And such association with these people created controversy among the teachers of the law, such as the Pharisees, at that time.

"He said, 'Those who are well have no need of a physician, but those who are sick; I have come to call not the righteous but sinners.'" – Mark 2:17

Jesus tells us with His own lips exactly the reason why He hung out with sinners, prostitutes, and tax collectors. Being immersed in sin is sickness, and that requires spiritual healing that only God can provide. Because of His divine nature as an ever-loving and a forgiving God, absolution of our sins is manifesting His glory. We are flawed, but we are cleansed when we repent and receive and live God's Word.

Life can be hard and tough, and being at peace amidst our own chaos can be challenging, in and of itself. God made it clear that His divine power is available to us should we choose to reunite with Him such that He can take over and be in control. And when we become messy within ourselves, it's next to impossible to help others.

Offering everything to God gives us ample space to receive more, so that we can give more. Ego and pride separate us from God's plans, and unless we're willing to let go of those, there's no space left to receive God's gift to bear much fruit and become His disciples to others.

By merely accepting the fact that we are far from perfect is already a sign of humility. The only perfect is God, and we can never be like Him. Our salvation is made possible when we accept His offering of a new relationship with Him through repentance and fellowship.

No human being can ever be qualified for God's calling, but He calls us for a divine purpose. Your flaws and my flaws are used for His Glory to lead others to God. It has been said that He calls the unqualified and He qualifies the called.

"You did not choose me but I chose you. And I appointed you to go and bear fruit, fruit that will last, so that the Father will give you whatever you ask him in my name." – John 15:16

In our time today, we witness conversions of convicted criminals and murderers who are now preaching God's Word. In fact, some of them have built their respective Christian congregations, highlighting how God's grace changed their lives. These real-life testimonies are not new to us, as we go back to the stories of people in the Holy Bible who also became witnesses of God's kingdom.

God's Not Done with You

Happy Birthday!

Yes. You read it right. Happy Birthday! The fact that you're reading this means you're still alive.

Every day is a celebration of life, with a glimmer of hope. You're still breathing, and God is not done with you yet.

There's a dispute in my one side of the family. It's so complicated that it called for a division among some members. It's both painful and depressing.

I talked to God one night in prayer, asking Him, "What do you want me to learn from this?"

I tried to find the answers from my own understanding, but I failed.

I realized that God has been giving me His answer all along, but I'm not listening. Because I'm too distracted, I can't hear His voice.

I recently bought a medical workbook online for a course that I'm creating; there's a tiny bookmark inside that book with the resurrected image of Jesus Christ, containing large texts at the bottom, saying, "I AM WITH YOU ALWAYS."

I reflected upon that. It dawned on me that I shouldn't be looking for answers anywhere else, because His Word can be found in the Holy Bible. And that's how I started to read biblical passages more often than I used to. I have a more intimate relationship and knowledge about Him now as compared to before, and it gives me a reassurance of who God really is that I serve.

You may be in a difficult predicament at this time. In fact, your tribulations and sufferings can be your purification period to mould your character in preparation for things greater than you've ever imagined.

You're not a hopeless case. God can use your brokenness to reveal His goodness. Because there's a more reassuring statement here: God isn't done with you yet. Although you're still a work-in-progress, you're His most precious masterpiece.

THE SINS OF COMMISSION AND OMISSION

"Anyone, then, however knows the right thing to do and fails to do it, commits sin." – James 4:17

Disobedience to God, big or small, is a sin. No exception.

Whether you stole one cent or one million dollars, it's still stealing. You still violated God's commandment.

This is where we really fail. Many of us—myself included—tend to justify our wrongdoings. Just because the intention is good, doesn't always mean it's godly and upright.

I'm guilty of this. Losing my temper is my common flaw whenever my children act out, especially in the midst of my household tasks.

I know of a depiction of an obvious sin but justified by many, because they said the benefits overshadowed the bad. Robin Hood's tales have been passed down for many generations. His persona was that of a destructive thief who would give money he stole to the poor people. The intention was good, but the means to help others was not godly.

So, how do we fight evil and not violate God's commands?

We commit sins through conscious knowledge; it's an act that requires participation by either ourselves or by others. And there are two ways how we, humans, commit sin:

First, through sin of commission. What it means is, we already know that it's a sin, and, yet, we still do it. In other words, it involves the willful act of doing something that violates God's commands in the Holy Bible, such as murder, stealing, and gossip, to name a few.

Second, through sin of omission. It involves not doing what is right or failing to do what God commands us to do, such as tithing, helping others who are in need, or failing to pray regularly.

And here's most of us have a problem with: sin of omission almost always leads us to sin of commission.

Let me elaborate more on that.

Helping Others to Grow

As parents, it's our primary responsibility not just to love and take care of our children but to help them grow as good and God-fearing citizens.

We are the leaders that they follow in their formative years.

In parenting, the values we instill in our children may vary due to preferences, lifestyles and cultural differences, but it doesn't preclude us from teaching them what's upright and what's not. In the eyes of God, sin is sin.

Serving others has been a Christian virtue. And Jesus became the perfect example of service when He washed the feet of His disciples during the last supper and when He gave His life in service to others through His ministry work before His death.

We are called by God to be His instruments of love, mercy, and service to others regardless.

"You shall love your neighbor as yourself." – Mark 12:31

If we are to follow Jesus, it's imperative that we do what He commands us to do.

It's easier to reciprocate what we've received. Realistically speaking, it's hard to love and forgive our neighbors, especially when the pain is inflicted by them. And that's exactly the example that Jesus showed us when He died on the cross.

"If you love those who love you, what credit is that to you? For even sinners love those who love them." – Luke 6:32

Our capacity to love as human beings is very limited. And our infinite source comes from God's vessel of love that never runs out. Because here's the thing: when we give Him all our love, we then become a receptacle of His love that will freely flow to others.

Helping others doesn't always necessarily mean giving something in kind, such as money or physical gifts. Although these are good things, sometimes others just need your presence, your time, your affirmations, your encouragement, or simply your hugs or your pat on the back.

Let others see the face of Jesus in us by helping them to grow in love.

Causing Others to Fall

When you hear believers leaving their faith, their respective churches and congregations or religious affiliations, what comes to your mind?

This is very common.

Although I can't be certain about the reasons of such separations in our time today, what I'm concerned about is this: it could cause others to fall and fail.

To fall and fail is to sin.

Remember our true purpose? To bear much fruit and to be God's disciples, right?

And I have this question to you: "Which punishment is heavier: to cause the fall of another person or when we sin ourselves?"

Sin is sin, which casts us away from God's kingdom and brings us to hell. It's like justifying lust as not a sin, because there's no tangible act of adultery.

"Whoever causes one of these little ones who believe in me to sin, it would be better for him to have a great millstone hung around his neck and to be drowned in the depths of the sea." – Matthew 18:6

It becomes even worse, because causing others to sin warrants severe condemnation, as the offender bears a bigger responsibility before God in the judgement day.

"That slave who knew what his master wanted, but did not prepare himself or do what was wanted will receive a severe beating. But one who did not know and did what deserved a beating will receive a light beating." – Luke 12:47-48

I know of a story of a married man who committed adultery. He left his family and formed a new one with this new partner. In the process, they had nowhere to go until a random woman welcomed them into her home to hide.

This woman must have known that it's not right to condone the wrongdoing. Instead, she became the instrument to perpetuate the sin.

One of the easiest ways to create a dispute between or among people is to gossip—the transfer of untruthful information about a person or an event. It ignites negative feelings of anger, frustrations, jealousy, and revenge, to name a few. It's the easiest and most common sin, and, yet, the gravity is intense.

"There are six things that the Lord hates, seven that are an abomination to him: haughty eyes, a lying tongue, and hands that shed innocent blood, a head that devises wicked plans, feet that hurry to run to evil, a lying witness who testifies falsely, and one who sows discord in a family." – Proverbs 6:16-19

CHAPTER 6

TRUST

W E HAVE ISSUES WITH TRUST ALL THE TIME.

Relationships are wrecked due to broken trust, which is evident among family members, friends, colleagues, politicians, and even in church.

It's our human nature that once trust is broken, to give or take it back is harder, which leads us to be selective of the people we hang out with. Feeling safe is a basic human need, which I've mentioned in the previous chapter.

You may have run out of people to trust, but there's only one with whom we can be sure that you're safe. His name is Jesus.

Trust is a core component of any relationship, and it has to be earned; it requires time and effort.

As a business owner, building good rapport with my clients is my main focus by earnestly working hard on the value that I provide through my products and services. When successful, gaining trust becomes easier. The harder part is to maintain that trust, so that they become my repeat and loyal customers.

In online marketing, I implement a process for a prospective client to buy my products and services through a seamless flow, called a sales funnel. According to experts, it takes a number of interactions before a prospect will buy from you. Although there's nothing set in stone as to how many times, but they would have to be exposed to your brand an average of seven times. And a properly set sales funnel can do exactly its job towards a successful sale.

For our discussion's sake, let me briefly describe what a sales funnel is.

In the first step, we do "prospecting". We then hook prospects in by bribing them with the so-called FREE stuff such as an e-book, cheat sheet, worksheets, or other freebies to build rapport. As we build rapport, we present our offer (our products and services). We can also answer objections, if needed. Then, we close the sale. If they're happy, they'll buy again and refer other people to you.

In other words, the customer has to find relevance in your business first with his or her needs, which then brings them to the next level. Once it's validated, then the rapport is built that triggers the prospect to give you his name and e-mail address. Because of trust, it then progresses to providing you with his payment information to complete the sale. When he's happy with the purchase, he may go back and buy again in the future, and, better yet, refer other customers to you.

This is the whole idea of the pyramid of trust we have among us today. To trust is to undergo a process.

The same idea is being taught to us as Christians. The foundation is laid for us by God. He revealed Himself as a faithful and living God, although we cannot physically see Him, but we can truly experience Him each time.

TRUSTING GOD

"Trust in the Lord with all your heart, and do not rely on your own insight." In all your ways acknowledge him, and he will make straight your paths." – Proverbs 3:5-6

How can we put our trust to God, especially when we have a pile of messy events in our lives?

What do we do to say we're trusting God? And what is trust, even?

According to Merriam-Webster Dictionary, trust is one in which confidence is placed. It also means to commit or place in one's care or keeping.

When God called me to write this book, I initially wondered why, but it makes sense to me now.

Life is full of surprises—good and bad—and God allowed them all to happen for a reason.

Having received a business lawsuit for the first time due to false claims by a certain party made me wonder and ask God, "Why? Is this part of Your master plan? What message would You like me to get from this?"

Again, this is on top of other challenges we handle at the same time. I have some moments where I'd like to just literally disappear.

"Can I finish this book some other time, Lord?"

I wish I can negotiate with God.

On the surface, it doesn't seem fair to me, but this book brought me to a different level of deeper understanding and consciousness in the spiritual realm.

My body, mind, and spirit felt weak, but I chose to trust God. I obeyed Him and committed to finishing this book. What amazes me though is, I feel a certain level of peace and joy amidst the present chaos in my life, because I've learned to believe in the mystery of His master plan for me.

As I gaze upon the snowy window pane one afternoon, God talked to me through the beautiful people seated right next to me at our kitchen table. I have four lovely children and a very supportive husband. I have a beautiful family!

"*When a woman is in labour, she has pain, because her hour has come. But when her child is born, she no longer remembers the anguish because of the joy of having brought a human being into the world.*" – John 16:21

God's Word gave me strength to continue in the knowledge that there's this great hope in Christ—deeper and wider than all of our dark days, for we know of the joy that's coming.

This book is my spiritual deepening and awakening—as God's means to properly prepare and equip me for a storm that He knew is forthcoming. He caused my spiritual alignment, as He knew I'm in the brink of getting derailed. He's moulding the character of a warrior under God's mantle of protection in me.

Helpful Truths About Trusting God

My current challenges may not be as intense as most of you have.

Different strokes for different folks, as they say.

Several months ago, I heard about a horrible story of a single mother whose three boys died of cancer, one after the other. And I have no words to describe that.

When we follow and believe in God, He doesn't promise that life will be seamless, pain-free, or perfect.

Trusting God is what we do when life seems hopeless and when we don't understand things from our perspective.

I run out of strength to open my mouth to pray, but trusting God is the only thing I can do, even if I can't grasp the turn of events and what's going on. To live and believe that God is in control requires trusting Him 100%, with no holds barred.

Examining my situation now—while God is asking me to do something for Him—brought me to seek God deeper to truly understand what trusting Him really entails. And I realized that:

1.**He knows me by name**. *"But now thus says the Lord, He who created you, Oh Jacob, he who formed you, Oh Israel: 'Do not fear, for I have redeemed you; I have called you by name, and you are mine."* – Isaiah 43:1

2.**He has plans for me**. *"For surely I know the plans I have for you, says the Lord, plans for your welfare and not for harm, to give you a future with hope."* – Jeremiah 29:11

3.**He has a divine purpose for me**. *"We know that all things work together for good for those who love God, who are called according to his purpose."* – Romans 8:28

Acknowledging God in Everything

To acknowledge God in everything is to recognize Him in all that we do, think, and say—not based on what our reasoning would be, but rather His divine character and what He can do for us in our lives.

The problem is, when we are faced with some difficulties, we tend to blame Him and curse Him, and then we turn our back on Him. And when things go the way we want them to go, we tend to forget and acknowledge that everything is because of Him.

I learned to acknowledge that, although He's not the author of our troubles and pains, He permits them all to happen to help us grow, learn, and mould our character in preparation for bigger things.

God doesn't owe us an explanation when life becomes painful and challenging.

The story of Job in the scripture would tell us exactly that following God doesn't assure us of convenience, problem-free life, healthy body, financial freedom, and whatnot. We may become the most faithful servant of God, but, on the other hand, we may also be suffering from all kinds of pain—based on the world's standards.

I've always wanted to win the lotto jackpot. Isn't it awesome? But I know I can never win because I don't bet. Kidding aside, there are true-to-life stories about lotto jackpot winners who have won huge amounts of money, only to be worse off than they were in no time. But, why? Because their financial mindset wasn't prepared for handling huge amounts of money.

I used to think that problems in our world today can be solved by money. And, yet, we hear famous individuals, successful people, and even celebrities commit suicide due to depression.

Although money is a tool that can be used to propagate God's works, money and God don't mix.

"No one can serve two masters, for a slave will either hate the one and love the other, or be devoted to the one and despite the other. You cannot serve God and wealth." – Matthew 6:24

When we acknowledge God in everything, we already have ourselves covered, because He can provide us with what we really need.

BELIEVING WITHOUT SEEING

"Have you believed because you have seen me? Blessed are those who have not seen and yet have come to believe." – John 20:29

I celebrated my fortieth birthday at the Holy Land in Israel years ago. We were able to personally see the Upper Room where the Last Supper had taken place. It was also in the same place where Jesus appeared to His disciples. What had really become significant in that event was when Thomas, one of Jesus's disciples, doubted His resurrection, telling the rest of the group that he'd only believe after seeing Jesus's wounds.

"To see is to believe" is one of the most common responses we'd give to people when they're trying to prove something to us. And it's very reasonable to not instantly fall prey to what has been said, because we need proof or evidence to support the statement.

In our Christian life, we know that God exists whom we believe in and pray to, even without fully comprehending. It's called faith.

Faith is both based on trust and on experience, because the reality is, nobody can place their confidence in someone or something he doesn't know at all.

You must have travelled via an aircraft in your lifetime. You boarded the plane, prepared yourself to be seated, and then fell asleep thousands of feet above the ground. Do you personally know the pilots? I bet you don't. But you put your full confidence in them, right?

The same is true for entrusting our health to medical doctors or relying our legal cases to our lawyers. We do all these things based on the belief and faith that they will just do fine.

Our faith in God is primarily based on two experiences: our very own and other people's personal experiences. We feel blessed when we experience His goodness and miracles personally as they do for others. We become the living testimonies and witnesses of God's works in our lives.

However, faith is a daily choice. With everything that's uncertain—except for taxes and death—we can only put our hopes to God to take charge and be in control of our lives. Faith doesn't need to have a rationale as to why you believe, because your full confidence is just there.

Knowledge, Belief, and Faith

We go to school to learn and to have knowledge about certain subjects that prepare us for the real world, because a measure of knowledge about something is essential to life.

As I've previously mentioned, our knowledge about God comes from our first church—our respective homes. Here, our family is our first ministry.

Knowledge goes with faith and belief to make up a solid trust towards a person or thing.

Faith and belief may mean the same in some aspects, but they essentially differ. In other words, while faith can include the element of belief, they're not the actually same.

One afternoon, my second child approached me with his frustrated aura, claiming that he was bullied at school. I asked him to describe the incident and what made him conclude of such occurrence. As a mother, I believed him, even without hearing what he had to say. Why? First, he's my son; I know him better than the other person. Second, his frustrations validated the claim. Third, it's a common event, especially at school. Although I may not have the strong evidence for the case, I just believed him, because that's what my mental assent told me. In short, I can say that belief is a product of the mind perceived to a certain occurrence coupled by the actions of the body.

Faith is something deeper, because it requires agreement of the spirit. It's beyond acceptance of the facts or what we superficially know. As Christians, we know that there's God; in short, we believe that He exists, although not every believer has faith in His divinity.

I can truly apply the difference of these to my own predicament at this time. I believe that God is all-time present with me as I go through this low season of my life and, at the same time, I have faith in Him that He will vindicate me and make me a victor and not a victim.

You see, it's a beautiful thing to align your mind, body, and spirit with God; your whole being is immersed in His presence to enjoy the peace and joy that only He can provide.

For us to trust God, it's essential that we all believe that He is the Living God and that He exists, which can then progress to faith, because true faith is more than simply believing; it's fully trusting with a change in our perspective in a different and godly way.

Keys to Build and Grow Faith in God

"So, faith comes from what is heard, and what is heard comes through the word of Christ." – Romans 10:17

We were all born naked—meaning, we didn't have anything with us when we came out from our mother's womb. We all started out from zero, although one may argue that some people were born into families with riches and fame and power.

Were you already talking on day one? Walking on day two? Reading on day three?

This just proves that we all have to develop a certain skill or a habit to progress to something new.

According to one of my personal development mentors, early childhood programming makes or breaks a person's outlook in life due to the different opinions and values thrown at him from his environment while growing up, which, in turn, becomes the huge deterrent towards discovering his true self.

I can attest to that. My late maternal grandmother commented that I could be a very good medical doctor, and that influenced me to aspire to be exactly that. Although I never became a medical doctor, my whole life was built on that one simple comment, because I believed in it. I trusted my grandmother's conviction, and I bought into it due to my confidence in her. That confidence had been ingrained in me, deep enough that it affected my life until now and why I ended up working in the medical field.

Our faith, be it either in our practical living or in God, has to come from somewhere. It comes mainly from what we see and hear.

"But it is in that way faith, comes from hearing, and that means hearing the word of Christ." – Romans 10:17

There are some basic elements or keys to build our faith over time.

First, faith requires an understanding not in the intellectual and corporal aspects, but in the spiritual realm. It also requires an active participation to make it alive. We are called to act forward into the unknown, believing that the Holy Spirit is leading us. Lastly, faith is a call for an uninterrupted obedience to God.

THY WILL BE DONE

Our very perfect model of prayer is The Lord's Prayer, highlighting very important key points, including the line, "Thy will be done on earth as it is in heaven." The Holy Bible is full of God's will, which basically just talks about our calling to fulfill His purpose for us, so that we become part of God's kingdom and family.

God gave us the free will to do whatever we want, but He also made it clear that there's a corresponding consequence to whatever we choose.

Because God knows our weaknesses and limitations that cause us to sin, He gifted us with the Holy Spirit as our guide to discern Thy will.

At home, we have our own sets of rules.

One day, my youngest child asked me, "Mommy, how come my classmate can watch TV after school?"

"My son, your classmate has a different set of parents who also has different sets of rules," I replied with confidence.

After that short conversation, he never asked me that question again.

As Christians, although God's will doesn't not necessarily mean rules, because we still have a choice to either do it or not, we need to know what this really means for us as believers.

So, what is God's will?

Knowing God's Will

I've previously mentioned that knowledge about God is imperative before we discern His will. And knowing God can be accomplished by knowing His Word.

"In the beginning was the Word, and the Word was with God, and the Word was God." – John 1:1

We used to have a pet dog, Whitey. Whenever he'd hear my father's whistle from afar, his tail would wiggle in great joy as he'd approach my father towards the door. He never missed a day. This was his routine. He knew my father, near or far. His whistle was his word.

I believe that knowing God's will works the same way. When we're familiar with His Word, we'd know His will. It comes in stages after knowing His Word. We can then walk with Him and develop a personal relationship with Him through prayer and consistent communication with Him. When we already built our relationship with Him, trust progresses; thus, we surrender our own will to His very capable and powerful hands.

As we walk in faith, obedience comes naturally, while we familiarize ourselves with His will. For instance, we know that stealing is wrong and because we know it's not part of God's design for you and me, we can easily denounce even just the thought of it. However, there may be times that we're still confused between two choices. God talks to us through our heart; He dwells in it. In the silence of your heart, guided by the Holy Spirit, know Thy will.

Apart from prayer, I'd ask advice from my most trusted spiritual mentors for discernment, because I believe that God talks to us through His people as well.

You may also want to examine the physical circumstances of your choice, as they can also leave a clue to know God's will.

Yielding to God's Will

If we are to define a perfect life, it would be next to impossible to do that, because there's no such thing as a perfect life—that's according to the world's definition of perfect.

The perfect kind of life is the life that's lived according to the will of God—a life that's in sync with Him. Here's the caveat: when we follow God, according to His will, it doesn't mean that it's pain-free, challenge-proof, or unflawed. But He promised this: "*Many are the afflictions of the righteous, but the Lord rescues them from them all.*" – Psalm 34:19

I know you'll agree with me when I say that it's hard to sometimes follow God's will.

Why is that?

Our technologically advanced world looks appealing and tempting. We are lured to pick up the shiny objects that we see, only to find out later on that they are harmful to our wellbeing. We tend to look on the surface and become fascinated by the external beauty instead of what's inside.

When I was a child, when given the opportunity to choose from nicely wrapped packages, I'd surely pick the big ones. But as I became older, I'd choose the smaller ones.

Why?

Women, are you with me? Although it's not always the case, smaller boxes, in my experience, would almost always contain more expensive gifts such as jewellery. As some say, "Good things come in small packages."

When there's a choice, it becomes difficult to focus on one. That's how our mind works as a human being. We're wired differently; we're prone to distractions, because we're always looking for something new, something that's odd, something exciting, something different. We're always curious. Although curiosity may sometimes be good, it led Adam and Eve to fall.

We're created to have body, mind, and soul in which the Holy Spirit dwells. Our physical body is God's extension of His ministry. It's used to perform the corporal works of mercy, such as feeding the hungry, clothing the naked, and visiting the sick.

When we don't take care of ourselves, how can we possibly take care of others?

God's will can also be manifested through our thoughts, and this is why we are encouraged to practice meditation on His Word to have that full understanding through the leading of the Holy Spirit.

"…for the weapons of our warfare are not merely human, but they have divine power to destroy strongholds." – 2 Corinthians 10:4-7

God and His Word are one, and His will is in His Word. When we are used by God to be His witnesses through our thoughts, He also uses us through the words that we speak.

Do your words bless or curse others? Do they inspire or discourage?

Because the reality is, we can't be full of faith if our thought processes are not permeated with God's Word.

We can also yield to God's will when we trust that His will is in our best interest. However, we have to remember that God's will doesn't appear before us automatically. We have to seek it out.

When we let God to be in charge and in full control over our lives, it will manifest obviously in the way we think, speak, and act. When there's transformation from the old self to the new one, we are on the path of fulfilling God's purpose to bear much fruit and be His disciples over nations.

CHAPTER 7

UNDERSTAND

WHEN I WAS PREPARING FOR MY MEDICAL SCHOOL YEARS ago here in Toronto, Canada, I was required to take the MCAT (Medical College Admission Test). The biggest challenge for me was the critical analysis/reasoning part, because this was based on reading and comprehension skills. What makes it even harder was, the questions were very tricky and answers seemed to be all the same.

So, what does it really mean to understand something or someone?

According to Merriam-Webster Dictionary, to understand is to grasp the meaning of something, to believe or infer something to be the case, and to accept it as a fact or truth, or regard as plausible without utter uncertainty.

In its practical application, to understand is to have a deeper sense of being empathetic towards a person or a situation without prejudgment.

To understand is also synonymous to, to empathize.

WALKING A MILE IN OTHERS' SHOES

I used to love online shopping, and the hardest part of it was the "one-size-fits-all description". For a person with special size needs just like myself, this won't be very beneficial.

However, there may be some things that can be applied to this description and, definitely, shoes can literally not be one of them. Shoes are very personal; when they don't fit, they don't fit. They can't be like a pair of pants or shirts that only need an alteration to fit.

What I really wanted to point out here is not literally the shoes that we wear on our feet; it's simply putting ourselves in someone else's situation, which requires understanding or empathy. It also means exhibiting compassion, which takes great emotional ability to be able to feel what others feel as our way of loving others the way God loves us.

"Rejoice with those who rejoice, weep with those who weep."
— Romans 12:15

We judge people easily, and I'm guilty of it—almost always. Whether we know them personally or not, we don't have the right to judge, because we don't know their full story or their sufferings.

In parenting, it becomes too common when different values are instilled. We can't really impose our own sets of beliefs on fellow parents for the choices they make, because we also don't know the options they are left with.

I chose to leave my corporate job and be a stay-at-home mom, and I'd hear some people questioning my decision. Others said that I was crazy to let go of my job while others are struggling to find one. Some commented that it's not practical, because I have four kids.

In a more serious sense, even suspected criminals have the right to undergo a fair trial and due process under the law until proven guilty.

"Whoever speaks evil against another or judges another, speak evil against the law ad judges the law; but if you judge the law, you are not a doer of the law but a judge. There is one lawgiver and judge who is able to save and to destroy. So, who, then, are you to judge your neighbour?" – James 4:11-12

Our Role Model for Compassion

"As God's chosen ones, holy and beloved, clothe yourselves with compassion, kindness, humility, meekness, and patience." – Colossians 3:12

Whether a person is a believer or not, nobody is spared from experiencing pain and suffering. We all travel the same journey— called life— in the same earthly path.

Temptations are everywhere, but God's goodness is manifested in everything. God blesses us through events, circumstances, or people.

"Mommy, can you staple this?" My youngest son approached me, handing me a stack of lined paper.

"What are you going to do with that?" I asked him.

"Oh, I needed to make a story book for my friend. She was sad yesterday," he replied.

My heart melted with joy and pride for my son. I envied his pure gesture of kindness and compassion.

What does compassion really mean?

We are all called to be compassionate in our Christian life, as we know that most of our brothers and sisters in Christ have different needs. And providing their needs doesn't have to be money-related all the time. But the problem with most of us—myself included—is that we tend to regard them as invisible. I know; I get it. You may say you're suffering, too. We all are, and God sees it. And that's exactly what being compassionate is all about—being there for others while you, yourself, are in dire need as well.

And it's not easy to become compassionate all the time. So, how do we do that?

When we don't know something, we look and ask for instructions—a guide, a map.

When we board an aircraft, the flight attendants teach us how to put our masks on in case of an emergency.

Jesus Christ does the same. He's the ultimate example of compassion and mercy. He stands as our perfect role model.

He demonstrated many examples of compassion during His ministry work, which you'd find in the Holy Bible.

Kindness is needed, but there's more to that. Compassion is one of Jesus Christ's qualities that we're called to imitate.

Let it be our goal to always have a compassionate heart like Jesus and be His vessel of love to bless others as we love ourselves as well.

Compassion for Self and Others

The best thing that we can give is love, as that breeds kindness, mercy, and compassion. I'm talking about the love that we can only find from One Source that truly suffices and never runs out: God's love.

If we have God's love in us, we can certainly give it to others as well. However, sometimes, we tend to take things out of context.

We are made to believe that when we think of ourselves first, it's demonstrating selfishness. God wants us to prosper; a prosperous spirit doesn't count whatever we give to others.

Being compassionate doesn't require us to give all our food to others while we have nothing left to feed our family and starve. Or being in the church the whole day while the children are left at home unattended. God is not pleased with that either.

We're actually missing the point.

"You can only give what you have." An old adage that truly makes sense.

To be able to be compassionate toward others, we need to be compassionate to ourselves as well. We have to forgive ourselves also. We need to love ourselves, too. Because if we don't, we'll surely feel burnt out, fed up, and exhausted. Our love tank will be empty, and there'll be nothing left for us to give.

If God's love is in us, then it becomes our nature to love others, too.

We know that Jesus talks in parables to share His message through a very practical lesson that every man can easily understand. One specific demonstration of compassion can be found in the Parable of the Unforgiving Servant from the Gospel of Matthew

18:23-35, which was about the story of a servant who owed his master an immense amount of money (talents) but was forgiven, and, yet couldn't forgive his own debtor.

What God is trying to tell us in that story is this: we should be merciful and forgiving to others because God has forgiven us, even if we don't deserve it.

ALL ABOUT EMPATHY

Compassion or empathy is a very noble effort, and just like any other talent or skill, it can grow if we're willing to do the work and share it.

Acknowledging that we—humans—don't naturally have it is the first step; meaning, we're not born with it and that somebody must have gifted us with that.

Empathy is God's gift. Everything is from God's provision and generosity. We are born naked, owning literally nothing. Some of us may have inherited fortune, name, or power, but think again. Where did these all come from?

After admitting to ourselves that we're nothing without God, we can truly say that we can't do things on our own; we need God. And like the talents we have, empathy grows when we share it.

Just like plants, empathy can massively grow when we nurture it. And we need God's help, coupled with our conscious awareness and selfless cooperation to do it.

Importance of Empathy

First and foremost, empathy is the face of God, a picture of God's great love for each one of us.

Demonstrating empathy to another person when you, yourself, are suffering is difficult, but God's grace enables us to do that.

When Jesus was hanging on the cross, He still prayed to God the Father for the forgiveness of our sins. I don't exactly know how to better articulate this kind of selfless act of a God to people who crucified and put Him to death. That's a real wow!

While most of us are pretty well-attuned to our own emotions and feelings, it's another story when we'd get into someone else's situation.

Whether you're a believer or not, it's crucial to understand why we have to demonstrate empathy to others.

First, because it's the right thing to do. Being able to put ourselves in someone else's situation and emotional state would enable us to extend our understanding by asking the question, "What if I'm in that situation?"

Second, it's important that we show empathy because that's what God wants us to do. It's God's will and purpose for us.

Third, when we share empathy, we grow in love for God and in God as well.

We are actually missing out on a lot of benefits by failing to show empathy. Remember, if you're not growing, you're dying.

The Dangers Without Empathy

All living things have the capacity to grow, be it physical or in other aspects of life. In the first place, living things are named as such because they have life. And for a life to grow, a conscious action has to be taken, because if not, it dies.

Although empathy is invisible, the same principle applies with it. It was freely given as a gift, and it has to be nurtured to be useful and serve its purpose. There are dangers in not being able to be empathetic towards self and others, which means it can be corrupted and wasted.

You'd agree with me when I say that everyone has loads to carry, burdens to bear. I have tons of them. But here's the thing: when we close ourselves off to being empathetic towards other people, we are also closing the door of empathy to ourselves.

"I was hurt before. I can't trust people again."

What about this one?

"I have to be very careful now, and I need to protect myself as I should."

Or these?

"If I do that, it may harm me, too."

"I'm afraid that I'll be involved. Let them suffer themselves."

When we do this, we are actually rejecting the gift.

You see, I can't honestly conclude or judge people's motives, but, for the most part, our human nature drives us towards becoming selfish and focused on our own best interest. Is it wrong? Well, that's where the mystery of God's will lies, especially when we are fully trusting God. Obedience requires following even without understanding it. And exhibiting empathy is one of them.

What God is telling us is, we can be other people's beacon of light only if we let God work through us.

When we refuse to exercise empathy, we also tend to manipulate the gift for ourselves. When we rely on our own understanding as to why we do the things we do—especially when they're not guided by the Holy Spirit—we miss out on our ability to read our neighbor's feelings and thoughts and regard ourselves as better than them. We tend to compare their comprehension about certain occurrences with ours, as we think highly of ourselves.

It can also lead to unhealthy relationships. When we put ourselves ahead of others, we lose sight of who we really God wants us to be. This usually happens when we expect them to return the favor, or we assume that the feeling should be mutual.

INVITATION TO THE HOLY SPIRIT

We know the truth that man can't survive on his own, because he has his own sets of limitations.

To be able to thrive, you and I need some help—a lifeline.

In business, it's recommended to leverage your resources by hiring people for some help to avoid exhaustion. However, this step should be taken cautiously to avoid problems in the future.

In my every effort to develop myself more, I joined a network that I initially thought fits my requirements. After paying my membership and attending meetings, I felt deep inside my conscience that something's not right. For that reason, I stopped showing up.

Some feelings of worry and anxiety sometimes do us good, especially when it entails compromising our values and whatnot. They also protect us from further engaging in temptations, thus protecting others, too. In doing so, we become more receptive and sensitive to the divine signs through our conscience.

God gave us our empathetic thoughts and feelings for a specific and divine purpose; it's a good idea to attune yourself to them, especially when it doesn't make sense.

So, what do we do when confused?

Invite our Holy Guide, the Holy Spirit. The good news is, it's readily available to us whenever we call. It's our access to God, 24/7.

Accessing our 24/7 Guide

One of the most important features in a product or a service is its customer support that we can access 24/7, especially when time zones become the primary challenge. It really turns me off when I have a concern, and somehow nobody is there to attend.

As a stay-at-home mom for several years now, it's reassuring for my children to know that they can access their mother anytime. When they left something at home that they needed for school, no problem; their mommy has them covered.

When a fellow mom needs some help, they can call on me anytime.

It's comforting in our awareness that whenever we are in dire need of something, there's a place to go.

The Holy Spirit is our spiritual support, with no waiting times. The moment we call, our line to God is instantaneously activated.

The Holy Spirit gives us the kind of wisdom we need to do things right.

CHAPTER 8

ACT

"For just as the body without the spirit is dead,
so faith without works is also dead."
– James 2:26

Making vision boards, goal-setting, journaling, reciting affirmations, and improving habits, are important to a person's pursuit to a successful life in the physical world.

Are these enough, though?

It's true that you can always hire a gym trainer, but you can't make him do the push-ups for you and develop the muscle that you want for yourself, because the thing is, you have to actually do the work!

For years now, I make my own sets of goals—both personal and business. One of my personal goals is to lose some pounds, but unfortunately, it hasn't been achieved as yet.

The same holds true for following God's will and being part of His Kingdom. Faith must be put into action for it to come alive.

MORE THAN WORDS

Men have different styles to pursue women in courtship. There are those who'd just talk with less actions, while others would simply show up and manifest their feelings through pleasing gestures and less talk.

As for me, I favor actions rather than words.

I remember this one guy who'd come to my school in university and show up out of the blue and wouldn't say much, except for some very basic words like "Hi, did you already eat? How's your day?" I could barely count the words coming from his mouth for a duration of about thirty minutes. However, he'd put in efforts by sending flowers, visiting my house, writing notes, and so on.

"So, faith by itself, if it has no works, is dead." – James 2:17

We must have heard this several times in sermons, recollections, retreats, and spiritual seminars.

Faith entails our ability to believe and must be acted upon, for it to come alive and work. Professing faith is not enough, and one must act on it consistently. Words and actions should go hand in hand. When our faith is dormant, God can't move in our lives; thus, we can't be His instrument to bless others, too.

Here's what I observe: some people are not just very articulate in expressing themselves through words, but when it comes to the actual job, they can deliver well with excellent quality.

I remember one time when I was a part of our company's job fair. We'd interviewed a young candidate whose resume was very impressive. However, during the interview process, due to a language barrier, this job applicant could not really express herself well. Unfortunately, she did not get the position. Because of that, I became skeptical about job interviews.

What is Your Doing Saying?

We always hear the old adage, "Actions speak louder than words". This is, for the most part, true. No matter how hard one tries to hide the truth, his actions will definitely reflect it.

Actions talk. Works are unspoken words.

We've had an issue with our first child during her teenage years; I believe it's very common to experience parenting challenges while raising a teenager. She would lock herself up in her room and wouldn't really talk to us, for the most part. I initially thought that uninterrupted doodling in her sketchpad was just part of her mood swings. It was then after some time that she expressed her deep enthusiasm for drawing and animation. Years went by, and she matured and pursued Animation in college. We're really proud of her, especially now that she has been accepted among thousands of applicants globally to be part of one of the best schools in Animation in the world, where Walt Disney and Pixar get their talents from.

It was just recently that we had the opportunity to ask her about what had truly transpired during those times, as we helped her recall the moment. We've determined that she was undergoing some identity crisis, and her drawings helped her to express herself.

Psychologists use drawings to assess their patients, as artwork can relevantly give clues about a person's emotions and feelings, past events, desires, ideas, perceptions, memory aides, et cetera.

My daughter's experience made me think and ask, "Why do I really do the things that I do now?"

The problem with most of us is, we ignore the reason why we really exist. Because of that, we miss out on the opportunity to fulfill our God-given purpose.

As a mom, whatever I do now relates to my family's best interest—my children's wellbeing, specifically. Live intentionally, according to God's will; it pleases Him.

Pleasing God Through Actions

You can't please everyone. It's impossible, no matter how hard you try.

While we believe that humanity came from one source, everyone is different when it comes to beliefs, values, preferences, lifestyles, and so forth. We are all born special; we have unique points of view about everything. And because of that, we tend to become critical of others when they don't agree with us. However, we should know that we can still agree to disagree, without hurting or manipulating anyone.

So, pleasing people shouldn't be our concern, because there's one more important thing than that: pleasing the audience of one—God.

Our earthly goals relating to success are not bad, but we should always be mindful about our ultimate goal to reach our final destination in God's kingdom. And to please Him requires conscious awareness and intentions to bring Him honor and glory and praise, which, of course, includes our relationship with others through the gifts and resources we were given such as time, treasure, and talent.

So, how do we please God?

To please is an action word. It means that we have to act and do something to make it happen.

Take to heart the first and greatest commandment of all, according to Matthew 22:37, *"You shall love the Lord your God with all your heart, and with all your soul, and with all your mind."*

Of course, when there's first, there should be second, and here it goes: *"You shall love your neighbour as yourself."* – Matthew 22:39

To apply these two greatest commandments, let me elaborate some examples on how to please God.

I've mentioned our God-given purpose previously. When we pursue God's divine calling for us, it pleases Him. It massively affects our way of thinking in a godly perspective that results in harmonious relationships with God, ourselves, and others. The results are manifested in the person that you become as you are transformed to a new person under God's grace. When that happens, we become the vessel of God's love that naturally flows and positively impacts the people we meet.

When others become inspired by the actions that we do for them, they, too, become witnesses of God's goodness. It creates a domino effect. We all then become the disciples of Jesus in today's generation. We become a conduit of God's grace to others.

DISCIPLESHIP

"Go therefore and make disciples of all nations, baptizing them in the name of the Father and of the Son and of the Holy Spirit, and teaching them to obey everything that I have commanded you." – Matthew 28:19-20

I was born into a simple, middle-class family in a small town. My parents were actively serving our parish as volunteers, which then brought my older brother and myself to follow their footsteps.

I know that there's God who exists. I also know that He's everywhere, and prayer is my communication line with Him.

As I've already mentioned, I was actively involved in a Catholic Charismatic prayer group in 1991 when I was in high school. I improved my knowledge about God, which led me to opening myself more towards a personal relationship with Him. My faith grew in words but not fully in action.

"And he said to them, 'Follow me, and I will make you fishers of men.'" – Matthew 4:19

The Cost of Following Jesus

Apart from being a medical doctor, I also dreamed about becoming a journalist, which never came to fruition due to lack of resources and support.

I was drawn more to the former, which became my foundation towards being the person that I am today. After finishing my four-year, pre-Medicine program, I landed a job as a medical transcriptionist. Years ago, I've had the opportunity to pursue medical school through the help of the hospital and the physicians I used to work with. However, two weeks before the official start of school, God told me that it wasn't my calling. I dropped the idea and backed out. Suffering from Postpartum Depression in 2012 led me to leaving my corporate job that I loved and transitioning to being a stay-at-home mom. I started my own medical transcription business at home. I also became a certified life coach, teaching parents—especially moms, and women—about self-development, business, financial literacy, and more.

A medical transcriptionist's job is a combination of being a journalist (writing) while being in the medical field.

Looking back at my life now, God gave me something different but related to my original aspirations and dreams. I may have my own plans, but God has a higher purpose for me.

I get it now.

The cost of following Jesus may not always agree with what we've initially planned for our lives, because His plans are the best. And most of the time, we may have to endure pains and sufferings when we follow His leading.

"The kingdom of heaven is like treasure hidden in a field, which someone found and hid; then in his joy he goes and sells all that he has and buys that field." – Matthew 13:44

The above passage simply says that if we want to follow God, we should be willing to leave everything, give up all we have, and pursue God at all cost—no exception.

Discipleship requires 100% from our being, not 50% or even 99%; it's either you're all in or you're totally out.

In other words, following Jesus may cost you everything, but it's all worth it.

Basic Principles of Discipleship

Being a disciple would mean being able to follow; and when we follow, it means we have a leader. As Christians, Jesus is our best example to follow—our best leader.

As humans, who are prone to being sidetracked by distractions and temptations, it's important that we focus on the one who gives the divine instructions. Here are some basic principles of discipleship:

First, we must wholeheartedly reconcile and restore our relationship with the Risen Lord. In doing so, we should be reminded that our motive to proclaim His name is to increase Him and to decrease ourselves.

Divine wisdom is a gift, and not everyone gets it right. As we become God's mouthpiece to spread the Good News, teaching it is an obvious element of discipleship. We have the responsibility to lead others to God and warn them when distracted, and it's our moral obligation to do something when this happens. Knowing God's Word will surely assist us in acquiring God's wisdom to lead others His way. Somehow, because we still have the human nature, we will try to do things our way and our own rationale may affect our leadership ability, which may also lead to conflicts. People don't like to be corrected; and addressing issues can be dealt with, with a spirit of love and gentleness.

Following Jesus also requires us to have our spiritual growth rooted in His teachings.

As a parent, I stand as my children's teacher, which works the same way with becoming a spiritual parent to others. As we feel delighted to see our children exhibit their developmental milestones—from crawling to standing up, to being able to feed themselves on their own—is the same idea that we want to do with spiritual parenting. We teach others to not be dependent on us all the time, knowing that God and only God can supply all our needs.

Being a disciple goes with the understanding that life is not a bed of roses all the time, and following Jesus is not a guarantee of a pain-free kind of life. We are called to set aside the worries of the world, so that we can focus on the heavenly reward.

It's our human nature to become comfortable of the things we know, but when we spiritually grow in God and for God, we realize that we need Him more. Discipleship entails dependence on God and not on ourselves.

THE DIVINE PARTNERSHIP

"For we are God's servants, working together; you are God's field, God's building." – 1 Corinthians 3:9

Doing stuff my way was already a thing in the past when I got married. As a wife, I must run all my decisions by my husband for his consideration. Decision-making, big or small, is something my husband and I equally share, and that's called partnership.

Married or not, all of us need a partner in something to come up with a sound decision or to get things done appropriately. And we can't just give our full trust to anybody or a stranger, but most of us have a handful of our trusted people to begin with.

In the business world, a partnership can also be set up as a legal relationship among stakeholders as business co-owners who share responsibilities such as financial, skills, and other resources.

Partnership generally requires involvement of two or more people who work together as a team towards a common goal, because it empowers all parties involved.

Experiencing the lowest point in my life at the present time, the most empowering partnership so far is my divine partnership with God. He is seated on the highest throne, and He can see everything from His point of view. It strengthens me to know that I have His back; it encourages me to go on.

Partnering with the Sovereign Advantage assures me access to the unlimited flow of divine wisdom for continued guidance and practical application in all areas of my life and the lives of others around me. When we take pleasure in God's business matters, we are assured that He walks with us. His divine and supernatural signs and wonders will be revealed, with favor flowing upon us.

Hitting my rock bottom allowed me to see the supernatural breakthrough available to me. Permanent partnership with Christ builds that supernatural confidence that I'm able to conquer any kind of setbacks.

"I consider that our present sufferings are not worth comparing with the glory that will be revealed in us." – Romans 8:18

Harvest vs. Laborers

We feel grateful for everything we receive from God, and that includes the results of our labor—both tangible and intangible.

I came from an underprivileged family, with little-to-no resources to begin with. People who know me well then can now appreciate my progress and achievements thus far. They'd go on to say that I'm now harvesting the fruits of my labor.

In our society these days, we associate harvest with material prosperity, which is not really bad. Of course, we need to seek growth to survive in this fast-paced world. However, I believe that, when we focus on our material prosperity alone, it masks our spiritual prosperity and our fellowship with God.

"The harvest is plentiful, but the labourers are few; therefore, ask the Lord of the harvest to send out labourers into his harvest." – Luke 10:2

The above biblical passage simply means that God has already won our battle; He already redeemed the world and the fruits of God's saving grace through His love and mercy are already available for us to enjoy and share.

God is inviting us to bring others who are lost to also enjoy the harvest, because many are still suffering and desperate for an answer and we have that answer ready to be shared.

CHAPTER 9

LOVE

"Beloved, let us love one another, because love is from God; everyone who loves is born of God and knows God. Whoever does not love does not know God, for God is love."
— 1 John 4:7-8

LOVE IS THE UNIVERSAL LANGUAGE. IT KNOWS NO COLOR, nationality, gender, age, education, or status. It's readily available to all.

JOHN 3:16

It's the most well-known and most often memorized verse in the entire Bible. It simplified everything about God's love, telling about the GOSPEL.

G – God sent His
O – Only Begotten
S – Son, that whoever believes in Him will not
P – Perish but will have
E – Eternal
L – Life

John 3:16 is the most comprehensive explanation I can find to describe the most beautiful kind of love that God has for you and me.

The Good News is in the GOSPEL, and it says everything about God's love.

THE NEWEST COMMANDMENT

"I give you a new commandment, that you love one another. Just as I have loved you, you also should love one another. By this everyone will know that you are my disciples. If you have love for one another." – John 13:34-35

To actually love everyone, including our enemies, is really, really difficult. It absolutely requires supernatural strength to do that.

The pains, sufferings, and death of Jesus on the cross clearly demonstrated the greatest love that ever existed in the history of the world.

We're told that if we don't love, we don't know God, because God is love.

CHAPTER 10

UNDER THE SON

I THOUGHT I KNEW GOD ALREADY, BUT I'M MISTAKEN—NOT UNTIL I reached my lowest point. This book showed me exactly who He truly is. This event felt like a spiritual renewal and revival for me.

I learned how to really surrender everything: my life, my future Under the Son—Jesus Christ.

DISCERNMENT AND OBEDIENCE

I feel pressured to be successful by fulfilling my goals and dreams in no time.

Setting goals is not bad, and acting upon them is not bad either. However, I felt I'm way too focused on the worldly definition of success, and God allowed me to be knocked down temporarily to remind me of His true purpose for my existence.

As I was preoccupied to win the game of life, I became distracted, ignoring my zeal for my true mission.

I admit that I must have overdone things in a short period of time, which I believe is akin to becoming misaligned with God's will. The teachings of the world promote idolatry rather than focusing on God as our only source.

Bishop Robert Barron, in one of his teachings, said that bad worship hurts us, because what we focus on outside the will of God will surely affect what we believe in,... so much so who and what we worship. Wealth, power, and fame are not really bad things, but do they actually bring me closer to God's purpose for me?

Bishop Robert Barron also expounded on these two things: "Religion of Grace" and "Religion of Karma."

God operates on the Religion of Grace, which simply means that there's nothing else you can do to change God's love for you. Salvation is already done for you, as He already paid the price.

Religion of Karma simply means you'll reap the consequences from your thoughts and actions—bad results from bad thoughts and actions, good results from good thoughts and actions.

"The Spirit has explicitly said that during the last times some will desert the faith and pay attention to deceitful spirits and doctrines that come from devils..." – 1 Timothy 4:1

Due to this modern-day concepts, beliefs, and practices that lead to confusion, seeking God's wisdom through discernment is a must.

What I'm going to say next may provoke an uncomfortable feeling of aggravation, displeasure, or disagreement. Due to peer pressure and the demands of life, I was made to believe and even participate in the New Age spirituality and its practices that most self-help books and teachings by famous gurus introduce, promoting oneself as divine by the use of mind power and other medium for channeled spirituality.

I realized that the seemingly unfavorable events in my life at the moment are God's most vivid way to redirect me to the right path and be back to His home again where I truly belong, as His way to protect me from further harm.

Through the Holy Sacrament of Confession, I was able to reunite with the Only One and True God. It also enabled my Catholic faith to be strengthened even more. I now renounce my involvement in any false doctrine or anything that is outside of God's teachings, such as yoga, Reiki, energy and vibration healing, chakras, meditation, (except for Christian meditations), law of attraction and cosmic power that claims the universe as the source, and the like.

"Your word is a lamp to my feet and a light to my path." – Psalm 119:105

I praise and thank God for this gift of spiritual alignment. I'm home at last again.

NO OTHER WAY

There's no other way but through the Son, Jesus.

"I am the way, and the truth, and the life. No one comes to the Father except through Me." – John 14:6

When we repent, confess our sins, and reunite with God, we become part of His kingdom and family, making all of us brothers and sisters in the name of our Lord Jesus Christ.

Vine and Branches

"I am the true vine, and my Father is the vine-grower. He removes every branch in me that bears no fruit. Every branch that bears fruit he prunes to make it bear more fruit." – John 15:1-2

My supernatural strength comes from God through His Son, Jesus. When I look upon the cross, I see redemption and freedom, feeling assured that everything is already paid. When I increase God in me, I decrease my dependence on myself. With that reminder, I feel empowered and more inspired to do things God's way.

My friend, the devil rejoices when you doubt God and hopes that you'll never find your way back home. You may be in the midst of a storm just like myself, but I'm truly convinced that God is up to something bigger for you. He has already made massive changes in me, and I can't wait to reveal it to the world soon!

When you pursue the Giver and not the gifts, you allow Him to transform you with spiritual maturity and wisdom. He'll use your story of victory to bless others, too. Remember that all things work together for good for those who love Him, who are called according to His purpose.

Living Testimonies

I have interviewed some women about their turning point and how God changed their lives. Here are some of them:

Year 2016 was the turning point of my life at age 55. In Canada, there's what we call "Freedom 55" that promotes financial freedom at 55 years old. Ironically, I was 55, but I was jobless, broke, and sick. I felt depressed, but I held on to God's Word in Deuteronomy 31:6 that says, *"Be strong and courageous. Do not be afraid or terrified because of them, for the LORD your GOD goes with you; He will never leave you or Forsake you."* I started to believe that, when I am down to nothing, GOD is up to something. He turned things around for me from being jobless into a blessing. I am now learning new skills and taking courses that will help me become my own boss.

– Sherry Lacson-Tan

It was in June 1992 when my husband left the Philippines to work in Riyadh, KSA. I was then pregnant with our second child. Being apart from him made me pray more and found myself going to mass daily. When I attended the Catholic Life in the Spirit Seminar, I grew my Catholic faith and learned the importance of participating in the Holy Mass. I also felt God's real presence during Adoration before the Blessed Sacrament. The biblical passage helped me from Psalm 46:10 that says, *"Be still and know that I am God."* It became alive in me, which now gives me the joy and peace in my life.

– Susie Par

"Welcome to Canada!" These three words echoed in my mind as the immigration officer stamped my visa. I felt happy and scared at the same time. After several years, I got married and now with two beautiful children. I'm currently a real estate investor and an entrepreneur while having a full-time job. God helped me through difficult times, and I held on to His promise. *"Trust in the Lord with all your heart, and do not lean on your own understanding. In all your ways acknowledge him, and he will make your paths straight."* - Proverbs 3:5-6

– Carlita Ilano

A few years ago, my mom got really sick in the Philippines while I was working in New Zealand. Being away from home left me anxious all the time. My mom is my "emotional why." My deepest frustration was not being able to be with her and my family due to my work overseas. I sought God's wisdom through Bro. Bo

Sanchez at the Feast, *"For you were called to freedom, brothers. Only do not use your freedom as an opportunity for the flesh, but through love, serve one another." –* Galatians 5:13. Subsequently, I embraced the world of entrepreneurship and built our family business. At this time, I'm enjoying my life with my husband traveling all over the world and seeing my mom more often while running our businesses.

– Crestine Carson

I lost my corporate job in Canada and felt helpless, but I trusted God. While searching for a new job, I used this opportunity to work on myself. I found a new job and also successfully obtained my Canadian citizenship. Everything fell into place. I realized that, amidst adversities, God is there to give us peace of mind. Hard work and persistence are the main ingredients, coupled with prayers, in achieving any goals in life. There will be some detours, but I know that they are just to redirect us to a better place. *"Many are the plans in a person's heart but it is the Lord's purpose that prevail."* – Proverbs 19:21

– Livinia Caviteno

While this whole book is in the editing stage, I received a phone call from our lawyer to prepare our case against our staff who took our money from one of the rental properties we own. Despite our every effort to connect in the past through e-mails, text messages, and phone calls, we were still ignored by our offender. I told the law firm that we'd like to give that person one last chance before an ultimatum is given and officially file the case before the court. Minutes after the e-mail was sent that same day, this person responded and agreed to settle with us amicably outside of court. Although in staggered payments, the other party was able to give us a portion of what's rightfully ours and promised to fulfill it until fully paid. Praise be to God! *"Good and upright is the Lord; therefore, He instructs sinners in the way. He leads the humble in justice, and He teaches the humble His way."* – Psalm 25:8-9

– Anna Santos

HIS AMAZING GRACE

I've gone through a lot of rough times in my life, be it in relationships, financial, health, personal, and spiritual.

God's amazing grace is the real deal that revives me each time I fall. I make my life as a living testimony of His goodness. The God I serve is truly alive. He reveals who He really is during the heaviest storms of my life.

I now completely dedicate my whole being to believing and worshipping only One God, as His amazing grace is experiential in my life through the seven sacraments of the Catholic Church towards a life in sync with Him.

I depend on God's leading; I even asked Him to reveal the title of this book to me.

A Woman's Amazing Grays
How to Age Gracefully with a Life in Sync with God

I'm physically aging, as evidenced by my gray hair, which multiplies by the day. But I'm not worried anymore, because I'm now dedicated to aging gracefully by being SPIRITUAL with a life UNDER THE SON, Jesus.

I will let the Son re-arrange my body as the temple of prayer to bring me the true fulfillment, joy and peace that I've been longing for.

"And the peace of God, which surpasses all understanding, will guard your hearts and your minds in Christ Jesus." – Philippians 4:7

There can never be any other kind of life as perfect as a life in sync with God.

I praise and thank Him for my spiritual awakening and alignment through my real-life experiences. I can tell you right now that our pains and sufferings are not punishment but rather God's protection from further harm, because He loves us so much.

To you, my dear brothers and sisters in Christ, I hope and pray that you are blessed by this book. I invite you also to become God's witnesses by sharing the message through this book to others. And thank you for being a part of my journey.

If you wish for me to speak at your events or provide you with group or one-on-one coaching on several areas like personal development, financial literacy, entrepreneurship, online marketing, and divine spiritual awakening, to name a few, you can connect with me at:

Website: **annasantoshub.com**
Email: **info@annasantoshub.com**
Alternate e-mail: **annasantoshub@gmail.com**

AMAZING GRACE
By Hillsong

All these pieces, broken and scattered
In mercy gathered, mended and whole
Empty-handed, but not forsaken
I've been set free; I've been set free.

Amazing grace, how sweet the sound
That saved a wretch like me, oh
I once was lost, but now I am found
Was blind but now I see

Oh, I can see you now
Oh, I can see the love in Your eyes
Laying yourself down
Raising up the broken to life

You take our failure; You take our weakness
You set Your treasure in jars of clay
So, take this heart, Lord; I'll be Your vessel
The world to see Your life in me, oh

Amazing grace, how sweet the sound
That saved a wretch like me, oh
I once was lost, but now I am found
Was blind but now I see

Oh, I can see You now
Oh, I can see the love in Your eyes
Laying yourself down
Raising up the broken to life

"Let NOT fear stop you from being the best version of yourself and fulfilling your God-given purpose." — Anna Santos

ABOUT THE AUTHOR

Anna Santos

Website: annasantoshub.com
E-mail: info@annasantoshub.com
Alternate E-mail: annasantos2910@gmail.com

Anna is a medical laboratory technologist by profession and a medical transcriptionist for over 20 years now. She built her medical transcription company in 2014, Trans-ACTS & Communications, that serves healthcare professionals globally. Her business extended its services to diversified customers in the legal field, academics, media, authors, and business owners of all trades and sizes.

She's dubbed to be the "Serial Mommy Entrepreneur" who runs several businesses in the comfort of her home, and received nominations and awards for such. She had been featured in media and local magazines as well, including the Canadian Real Estate Wealth Magazine. She finds balance and happiness in all that she does, which she now willingly shares to others globally through her speaking engagements, personal coaching, self-development programs, and the articles and books she had written and plans to write in the future.

She also had the opportunities to share the stages and co-author books with the legends such as Brian Tracy, Jack Canfield, Kevin Harrington, and many other prolific speakers.
Connect with Anna now!

Anna Santos
Making Things Happen.